Making Dyslexia Work for You

Second edition

**Vicki Goodwin
and
Bonita Thomson**

Routledge
Taylor & Francis Group

LONDON AND NEW YORK

First published 2004
by David Fulton Publishers

This second edition published 2012
by Routledge
2 Park Square, Milton Park, Abingdon, Oxon OX14 4RN

Simultaneously published in the USA and Canada
by Routledge
711 Third Avenue, New York, NY 10017

Routledge is an imprint of the Taylor & Francis Group, an informa business

British Library Cataloguing in Publication Data
A catalogue record for this book is available from the British Library

Library of Congress Cataloging in Publication Data
Goodwin, Vicki.
  Making dyslexia work for you / by Vicki Goodwin and
  Bonita Thomson. – 2nd ed.
  p. cm.
  Includes index.
  1. Dyslexics – Education. 2. Dyslexia. 3. Study skills. I. Thomson,
  Bonita. II. Title.
  LC4708.G66 2012
  371.91'44--dc22   2011013342

ISBN: 978–0–415–59755–5 (hbk)
ISBN: 978–0–415–59756–2 (pbk)
ISBN: 978–0–203–80311–0 (ebk)

Typeset in Helvetica Neue
by Florence Production Ltd, Stoodleigh, Devon

MIX
Paper from
responsible sources
FSC® C004839
www.fsc.org

Printed and bound in Great Britain by
TJ International Ltd, Padstow, Cornwall

Contents

CONTENTS

PART 3
Resources for you   **167**

APPENDICES

Acknowledgements

We would like to acknowledge all the wisdom and experience that so many dyslexic adults have generously shared with us.

We would like to thank the many colleagues from whom we have learned so much over the years.

Our thanks also go to our long-suffering partners for their patience and encouragement.

Some of the activities, strategies and illustrations in this book first appeared in the *Dyslexia Toolkit* (Goodwin and Thomson 1999), funded and published by the Open University.

Vicki Goodwin wishes to thank the Open University for allowing her time to read and research for the first edition of this book (2004).

We are indebted to Jennie Lee for allowing us to include on the website her spelling programme, MUSP, adapted for use without a tutor.

Introduction

When we first thought about writing a book for dyslexic adults we seriously wondered if we were doing the right thing. The first edition proved to be so popular that we have expanded and updated it to include two additional chapters covering self-esteem and what family and friends can do.

Not everyone gets help when they need it. This is a book to help you. You can dip into it and come back to it as often as you need. We hope it will stimulate you to try some of the ideas and create more of your own. We really want you to discover things for yourself because these are the things that usually work best; many of the ideas and strategies included have been devised by dyslexic adults.

If you know very little about dyslexia, then start at the beginning. Part 1 covers some of the things we now know about the dyslexic brain and the range of associated difficulties and strengths.

Part 2 is your 'toolbox'. If you don't know what you are looking for, you can move through the headings until you find what interests you. It introduces a variety of strategies for you to build on and develop for specific situations:
- the world of print;
- written communications;
- planning and organization;
- numbers and memory.

Part 3 is about resources and how information technology (IT) can help. It also explores some wider issues about dyslexia in daily life, especially education and the workplace.

We hope that your family, friends, tutors and employers will also find the book useful.

Using our website

Our publishers have an online resource. We have used this for:
- printable documents;
- expanding on some of the topics;
- other useful information.

We indicate in the margin where there is additional material available. You can find the online resource at: www.routledge.com/textbooks/9780415597562.

Printable documents

Throughout the book we have included short activities to get you thinking about how you do things and what you might need. You can complete these activities in the book or, for some of them, you can print the page from the website.

There are also printable documents of useful information not linked to activities such as the alphabet arc and the multiplication tables square.

PART 1

Dyslexia and you

There are four chapters in Part 1:

- Chapter 1
  Finding out about dyslexia and the brain
  What we know about dyslexia and the brain

- Chapter 2
  Exploring your dyslexia
  *What dyslexia is, and feelings about being
  dyslexic*

- Chapter 3
  How dyslexia affects you
  Considering your dyslexia and your needs

- Chapter 4
  Support from those close to you
  How family and friends can give effective help

Although you don't *need* to read Part 1 first, you will find something here to get you thinking about how dyslexia affects you. We help you to understand what is happening in your brain and identify your strengths. Armed with this knowledge you can move confidently on to Part 2.

1

Finding out about dyslexia and the brain

Understanding something about dyslexia will help you to know what might be going on in your brain.

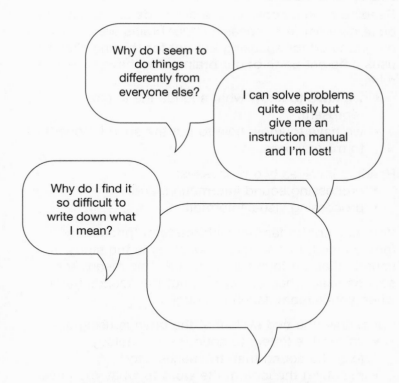

Why do I seem to do things differently from everyone else?

I can solve problems quite easily but give me an instruction manual and I'm lost!

Why do I find it so difficult to write down what I mean?

Do any of these ring a bell? You might like to add a comment about yourself.

Dyslexic brains are different. That's official. There is scientific evidence to show that the dyslexic brain processes information differently. For example, with various brain-scanning techniques we can now see what is happening in our brains when we are doing particular tasks; the scanner measures which bits of the brain are active. We can see that dyslexic brains are active in a different way to those of non-dyslexics.

This chapter looks at how we read, write and use the English language, and at some of the scientific evidence for dyslexia.

How we read

Reading makes considerable demands on us that are quite different from speaking. Our brains are programmed for speaking but not for reading. Reading uses different parts of our brain so we have to learn the rules:

- we have to know what sounds the letters represent;
- we have to know how to put the sounds together to make words.

Reading involves two processes:

- processing sound information; and
- processing visual information.

You may not be familiar with the term 'phonology' (pronounced: fo-nol-ogy). Phonology is the study of sounds that are found in language. This means the sounds used when you *speak*, not the sounds made when you scream, laugh or cough.

Put simply, the two skills that the brain is using are:

- linking the letters to sounds – phonology
  (e.g. the sound that 'th' makes); and
- matching the look of the word to what you have seen before – visual.

ACTIVITY 1
Your difficulties learning to read

Can you remember learning to read? Can you remember having any of the following difficulties?

- Couldn't remember the different sounds of the vowels: a e i o u.
- Couldn't tell the difference between some letters such as 'p' and 'q', 'b' and 'd'.
- Had difficulty with pronouncing 'th' and 'f'.
- Couldn't remember the sounds for 'ough' in though, through, cough, enough, bough.
- Circle any of these words below that describe how you remember having felt at the time and add any others you think of:

  frustrated   angry   resigned   foolish
  perplexed   tired   embarrassed

These are the skills required for reading. Dyslexic people use these two skills in a different way to most people. If you want to know a bit more about how these work when we read, refer to the additional information: *How the brain reads* and *How we learn to read* in the *Reading* section of our online resource.

Figure 1.1 shows how the tasks are divided between different parts of the brain. You will sometimes hear reference to the 'left brain' (i.e. 'sound centre') and the 'right brain' ('visual-spatial centre') but both sides of the brain are involved in reading.

We have oversimplified the real situation. If your phonological processing (the 'sound centre') is inefficient then your visual processing (the 'visual-spatial centre')

```
┌─────────────────────────────┐
│     The Planning Centre     │
│  The front part of the brain: │
│   for planning, sequencing, │
│    change, new ideas and    │
│          attention          │
└─────────────────────────────┘
```

```
┌──────────────────────────┐   ┌──────────────────────────┐
│     The Sound Centre     │   │  The Visual-Spatial Centre │
│   The left-hand side of the │   │   The right-hand side of the │
│  brain: where sounds are  │   │ brain: where visual information │
│ processed – letters are linked to │   │ is processed and awareness of │
│  sounds and sounds to letters │   │      space is handled      │
└──────────────────────────┘   └──────────────────────────┘
```

Figure 1.1 Adapted from the model of Alan Baddeley (*Working Memory*, Oxford: Clarendon Press, 1986)

will make up for it. However, the visual route is slower. It is also hopelessly unreliable for reading long words and not good for new words. You probably have difficulty reading words you've never encountered before.

Look at the words on this list. Try reading them aloud:
- pathognomonic
- homunculus
- reafference
- diphenylbutyl

We can't check whether you've got them right but we suspect that you would struggle to read them straight off because they are probably unfamiliar to you. Are you beginning to understand how you read?

You may also have experienced muddling words that look very similar. Try these pairs:
- spilt *and* split
- affect *and* effect
- though *and* through

Look back at Figure 1.1. When you are reading, the 'visual-spatial centre' may let you down.
As you read through texts your visual-spatial centre:
- cannot recognize a word you've never met before;
- may mistake one word for another.

If your 'sound centre' works well, it will deal with these situations by recognizing the letter sounds and putting them together. This is called 'phonological awareness'. But, in dyslexia, the processing in the 'sound centre' is often very inefficient, so you have to rely more on the 'visual-spatial centre'. Reading, therefore, becomes slower and harder.

In summary:
- Phonology is about the way that speech sounds relate to letters.
- You need phonological as well as visual skills to read efficiently.
- In dyslexia, phonological skills (the sound centre processes) are usually underdeveloped.
- Dyslexics tend to use the slower, less reliable, 'visual-spatial' centre of the brain.

The sound centre: phonology and phonological awareness

Your phonological skills should develop *before* you learn to read. This is why learning nursery rhymes and tongue twisters are so important. There are 3 stages in the development of phonological skills. These are summarized in Figure 1.2 and explained below.

1.	Awareness of syllables *You beat them out*	rail-way foot-ball-er (footballer)
2.	Onset and rime *You learn tongue twisters and nursery rhymes*	b-ounce tr-ain
3.	Phoneme *You can hear the different sounds in a word*	sh-ee-p s-t-i-tch

Figure 1.2 Three stages of development
of phonological skills

Pause for a moment

With dyslexia, some or all of these skills are never fully developed.

- Can you beat out syllables correctly?
- Can you hear the difference in your head between the first sound of a word and the rest?
- Can you count the number of phonemes (the *sounds*, not syllables) in each word? Try counting the sounds in 'blue' and 'felt'. (b-l-ue has 3 and f-e-l-t has 4.)

If you want to check these skills, you can refer to the additional information on *Phonological skills* in the *Reading* section of our online resource.

The visual-spatial centre: recognizing words by sight

The right-hand side of the brain does much of the work when it comes to recognizing words by sight. This is very useful for those short frequent words we need, such as: the, and, a, it, no, not etc. The brain can get quite good at recognizing longer words too – particularly those that you use regularly. But the visual-spatial centre can get it wrong.

- It may not spot the difference: such as in 'registration' and 'resignation'.
- Or it may think it's guessing the right word when it is choosing a similar one: such as reading *identify* for *indemnify*, thus getting the meaning of the sentence all wrong.
- If concentrating very hard on decoding the words, it may miss some of the little words – like 'not' for example. Missing 'not' changes the whole meaning completely.

The dyslexic brain relies more heavily on the visual-spatial processing and is therefore more affected by these shortcomings.

Learning to read and write

The skills we need to learn to read and write are listed in Figure 1.3. Often all these skills may not be present or well developed in dyslexic children. And these difficulties can persist into adulthood.

Another way of illustrating this is shown in Figure 1.4; it is complex – you can begin to see why some people have difficulties!

If some of these skills are absent or poorly developed, the result is that learning to read and write becomes exceptionally difficult. You may have vivid memories of what it felt like.

- Reading is about *decoding* what's in front of you.
- Writing is about *coding* what is in your head.

If you want to think a little more about these skills then go to *Skills required for literacy* in the *General* section of our online resource.

Skills required to learn to read and write	Examples
Knowing the letters of the alphabet, what they are called	Being able to distinguish **b** from **d**
Recognizing syllables	Being able to beat out the number of syllables correctly
The linking of sounds to letters or groups of letters (phoneme knowledge)	Knowing the sound made by the letters 'ai', 'sch', 'ing', 'bl'
Ability to take sounds away from a word and know what sounds are left	E.g. what sound is left when you take the 'ch' sound from 'chips'
Holding sounds and words in the short-term memory	Putting together the sounds to make words and words together to mean something
Ability to pronounce complex words	Coping with words like anemone, specific, etc
Knowing the meaning of a lot of words	Having a good hearing vocabulary
Being able to recognize word sounds from other sounds	Such as knowing that they are words rather than rubbish

Figure 1.3 Skills we need to read and write

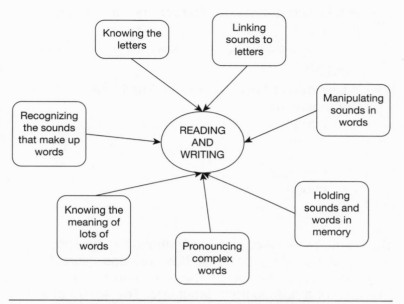

Figure 1.4 Skills we need to read and write

The English language

The English language presents additional problems for dyslexic people compared with a language such as Italian, for example. English is a 'non-transparent' language. This means that:

- sounds are not always represented by the same letters:

---

a

The 'long |a|' sound, as the word **bay**, can be written as in:
mate,
    bait,
        and the word 'a' itself.

- letters and groups of letters do not always sound the same:

---

ough

Just look at how many ways 'ough' can be pronounced:
    bough
    rough
    through
    thorough
    cough!

So this huge variation has implications for reading, writing and spelling for us all. It is very bad news if you are dyslexic. Italian, on the other hand, is an example of a 'transparent' language. The sound of a letter or group of letters never varies. Once you know how to pronounce each letter or group of letters, it's always the same.

So the English language is full of challenges. You will need, as always, to be creative with your learning. This is what Part 2 of this book is all about.

Inside the dyslexic brain

The study of the dyslexic brain and how it functions is part of the branch of science called 'neuroscience'. Since the 1990s there have been great strides forward in understanding how the brain functions generally.

The human brain has two parts called hemispheres, joined together near the middle. It is asymmetric: the right hemisphere is a bit smaller than the left. In the late 1980s work on the brains of dyslexic people showed that, compared to non-dyslexics, the dyslexic brain:

- is more symmetrical; there is less of a difference between the hemispheres; and

- has a different structure, including in the part that joins the two hemispheres.

During the 1990s there were great advances in scanning techniques that allowed scientists to watch which parts of the brain were activated when carrying out certain tasks. Scanning is a non-invasive way of watching how our internal organs, including the brain, are functioning.

As scientists gradually pieced together the evidence, it became clear that, in dyslexia:
- Left hemisphere language areas of the brain are less well developed.
- The areas of the brain involved in reading and writing do not work together as they should.
- The information flow between them is inefficient.
- Information gets jumbled up.
- Even in adults who now have few difficulties, their brains are processing differently to non-dyslexics.
- The structure of the brain is different.
- Tasks that you do automatically are affected – see information on *the cerebellum* in the *Science of dyslexia* section of our online resource.
- Fluency can be slow.

In the extreme, the evidence suggests that, for some people, words cannot be understood and spoken at the same time. This may explain why it is so difficult to read out loud; reading aloud means that you have to decode the word and then pronounce it. You also need to do several things at a time when making notes; you have to listen, summarize and write. Does this help to explain why you find some things difficult or impossible?

Visual sensitivity
Many dyslexics experience visual difficulties that do not seem to be corrected with standard spectacles. Print on a page, particularly black on white, is uncomfortable to

read. It can distort, swirl around, jump about and pulsate.

Some people get so used to it that they don't realize that it doesn't happen to everyone. Of course, it slows down the speed of reading and increases fatigue. There are some extreme examples of the way the brain can distort print information in Figure 1.5. Here are just two people's descriptions:

> When I read a lot, the print blurs and distorts. I was quite sceptical about coloured overlays but I find the yellow one makes a huge difference; the print is clearer and more stable.

> I find that changing the background colour of my computer screen to pink keeps the words still and I can read for longer.

For more information go to *visual discomfort and distortion* in the *Reading* section of our online resource.

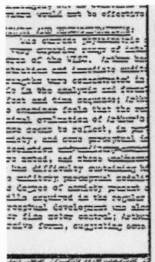

Figure 1.5

Genetics and dyslexia

Observations indicate that dyslexia seems to run in families. You may know of others in your close family with similar difficulties to you even though they may never have had dyslexia identified.

My Dad was really knowledgeable. He knew a lot about everything. He read books but took ages over them. He ran his own business and did very well but he hardly ever wrote a thing down. My Mum used to do all the accounts and write his letters until he got an accountant and a secretary.

My sister was just as clever as me but she was hopeless at exams. I went on to study science at university. She was dotty about animals and used to help the local vet, first on a voluntary basis, and then as a proper job. The vet had a lot of faith in her. She knew exactly what to do with sick animals but she couldn't be persuaded to train as a veterinary nurse. She said she was happy doing what she did and couldn't bear the thought of doing exams.

There is now a lot of evidence for a genetic connection for dyslexia – but not a simple one.

If you have a good scientific background, you might find this review paper interesting: 'Genetics of dyslexia: the evolving landscape' in the *Journal of Medical Genetics* in 2006, revised 2007, that can be downloaded from http://jmg.bmj.com/content/44/5/289.full.

In conclusion

So there are several scientific explanations for the problems dyslexics face. There are probably many different causes for dyslexia, which is why no two people have exactly the same profile of difficulties. Each of us has different strengths and attributes. It is these that help us to develop ways of dealing with the difficulties in different ways with varying success. This also makes dyslexia quite difficult to define. We like this definition for developmental dyslexia (dyslexia that has not been acquired through accident or illness), adapted from David McLoughlin:

> Dyslexia is . . .
> - a genetically inherited neurological difference that affects the efficiency of the cognitive processes underlying learning and performance
> - in conventional educational, work and life settings.
>
> It has particular impact on verbal and written communication, as well as organization, planning and adaptation to change.
>
> (After McLoughlin *et al.*, *The Adult Dyslexic, Interventions and Outcomes*. Whurr 2002)

The major advantage of recent advances is to show that dyslexia is very real. Many of you reading this book will have come across sceptics – people who think there is no such thing as dyslexia, that it's 'just a matter of applying yourself' and if you can't do it, then you're 'thick' or 'lazy'. Now you can say with confidence that dyslexia *is* real and that it is underpinned by scientific research.

Pause for a moment
We'd like you to reflect on this chapter and think about the following question.

> If science could produce a cure for dyslexia, would this be a good thing? Would *you* go for it?
> Are there any advantages to being dyslexic?
> Would society be poorer without dyslexic people?

In this chapter

In this chapter we've only been able to give you a very general overview. This means that some of the science is grossly oversimplified. If you have the time or energy you might like to follow some of this up. A good starting point is *Dyslexia in Context*, edited by Angela Fawcett and Gavin Reid (Whurr, 2004), which offers fascinating chapters on research, policy and practice.

2

Exploring your dyslexia

If you understand where you are you can at least aim for where you want to go.

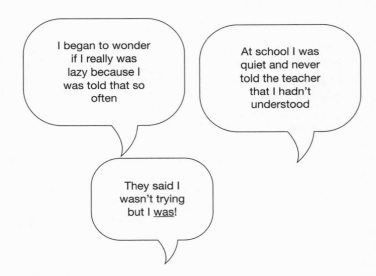

I began to wonder if I really was lazy because I was told that so often

At school I was quiet and never told the teacher that I hadn't understood

They said I wasn't trying but I <u>was</u>!

How does it feel to be dyslexic?

Some of the descriptions of how it feels to be dyslexic are about feelings of frustration. Reading and writing can seem incredibly difficult. Words can be hard to recognize and hard to use. Organization can be an issue too. Losing your way, trying to read aloud, struggling to keep up with work – all contribute to a general sense of exhaustion and lack of confidence. All this is about living in a world where most people are *not* dyslexic.

There can also be a different feeling, one of excitement, when everything seems to come together and you realize you have understood a situation or problem in a wholly unique and remarkable way. Tom West, in his book, *In the Mind's Eye* (see Appendix B) shows that many dyslexic thinkers have an unusual balance of skills that are often outstandingly creative.

 ACTIVITY 2
How does it feel for you?

Take a moment to think about how your dyslexia affects you. Think about the questions in Figure 2.1 – tick the answers that are closest to yours.

This may help you to think about what you want or need to do.

Do *you* think you are dyslexic?

You may be looking through this book because you have recently had an assessment that suggests you are dyslexic, or because you know someone who has. You may have had an assessment as a child and want to understand it better. If you are reading this because you are still wondering if you are dyslexic, have a look at the initial screening checklist (Appendix A) and read at least the last part of this chapter.

Effects of dyslexia

Almost everyone will experience some difficulties but people with dyslexia will encounter many, such as:
- reading, which is likely to be frustratingly slow;
- struggling with reading comprehension;
- concentration, which tends to fluctuate;
- spelling and grammar, which can be unorthodox;

What do you find most frustrating?	• Reading so slowly • Not being able to get down on paper what I want to say • Forgetting words or names • Having illegible or uneven handwriting • Misreading words • Not being able to spell • Not being able to find something • Being late • Anything else – what? _____ _____
How do you think others see you?	• Lazy • Creative • Disorganized • Untidy • Quirky • Intuitive • Inspired • Determined • Slow • Odd • Different • Extraordinary • Anything else – what? _____ _____
What are your particular strengths?	• Generating ideas • Thinking holistically • Solving problems • Being artistic • Being musical • Having empathy • Getting things done • Inspiring others • Reading maps and diagrams • Good at sport • What else? _____ _____

Figure 2.1

- physical co-ordination and handwriting;
- remembering information;
- organizing and planning;
- working within time limits;
- thinking and working in sequences;
- visual difficulties such as blurring and distortion of print;
- good days, bad days: inconsistency of what can be achieved.

All these difficulties make things worse or even impossible on a bad day. Inexplicably things just don't seem to fit together in your head, the connections don't get made. You can't seem to work properly at anything, yet the day before or even tomorrow things are fine.

How do people find out if they are dyslexic?

There are many ways in which people discover their dyslexia. Usually it doesn't come as a total surprise; it confirms something you have suspected for some time.

Suddenly I realized all these different difficulties were all connected. It felt like the final pieces in the puzzle had fallen into place. It explained so much.

The subject of dyslexia may come up in a number of different ways:

- **Your teacher** suggests you are dyslexic.
- **A member of your family** or someone else may suggest the possibility that you have dyslexia.
- **One of your children** may be assessed as being dyslexic and you recognize yourself in them.
- **At college or in the workplace** someone suggests dyslexia as being the cause of difficulties you are experiencing.
- **A news item** describes dyslexia in a way that rings bells for you.

A combination of some of these may gradually raise your awareness of dyslexia and you may decide to find out more. Let's look more closely at these through some personal experiences.

At school: primary school

In a primary school setting a teacher might notice that a child seems to be making inconsistent progress. An otherwise outgoing child may be slow in learning to read and curiously reluctant to read out loud. They may produce unusual spellings but appear highly articulate and able to grasp concepts quickly. Sometimes, at this stage, a child might be screened for dyslexia and given some additional teaching. In primary education a class tends to have the same teacher for all subjects so it is easier to be aware of the child who is having difficulties. But it is possible for difficulties of a very bright child or a quiet child to go unnoticed so long as their progress is average.

Here is one person's story:

I remember when I went to school I was very excited about the prospect of learning to read and write. I loved stories and books. I didn't realize for a while that I was having a hard time of trying to make sense of the letters and words until we began to read aloud and to read words that weren't in my reading book – I knew those off by heart.

When I started writing stories I had so much to say but the teacher marked almost every word wrong and told me I had to do something about my spelling. I felt crushed. My exciting story packed full of ideas didn't seem to count for anything.

I still hadn't managed to read properly by the time I was 9 and dreaded reading lessons because I was so slow compared with all the others in the class. Writing was even worse – I never seemed to

*complete anything. I can remember a lot of red
crosses and the critical comments on the bottom:
'you must make more effort.' But I thought I had!*

At school: secondary school

In the secondary school situation there is usually a
different teacher for most subjects. This can be hard
for everyone but can be additionally stressful for
dyslexics. It is much more difficult for teachers to spot
individual inconsistencies. Difficulties may not be noticed
or may be regarded as 'laziness' or lack of ability.
If they are picked up, then the young person may get an
assessment and some structured support. However, a
number of people get through the school system without
having dyslexia identified. They may get by on their
natural ability or wit, or they may be wrongly identified
as slow learners or disruptive pupils. For them a proper
assessment comes very late. As a result they may not
have been taught learning methods and study skills that
suit them. They probably won't have been taught study
methods that are appropriate for dyslexia. Despite
putting in tremendous effort they will have little to show
for it. Learning seems to be so difficult, giving rise to
considerable frustration and feelings of inadequacy.
It is not surprising that many are 'turned off' school and
learning.

Another dyslexic adult remembers:

*It was only in class discussions that I found I was
able to explain what I wanted to say and they realized
I had in fact understood a lot of what was being
taught. I could listen and understand, but
I couldn't write it down. I would get stuck on one
unfamiliar word and then lose the thread of the
sentence. I could write the homework down slowly
or get to the next class on time. By playing the clown
I managed to avoid some of the scorn.
I pretended that it was because I was scatty that*

*I forgot, was late, missed the homework etc. That
was a more acceptable label than 'lazy' or 'stupid'.*

*Every day there was something I had forgotten or
lost. One day it was my reading book and a note for
the teacher, another day my pencil case and bus
pass.*

Pause for a moment

Does any of what you have read so far chime for you?
You might like to highlight some of the words and
phrases in the experiences above that ring particularly
loud bells.

From your family or other people

Often a parent is concerned as to why their son or
daughter is struggling at school. They are not put off
by teachers' comments such as 'let's see how they go'
year after year. They start finding out a bit more about
dyslexia:

*As a parent I remember looking at my son's history
test when he was about 9. The teacher had marked
every single answer as wrong and put 0/10 at the
bottom but when I looked through the test I
recognized that he had got more than half the
answers right. He had misspelled 'battle' as 'battel'
and 'conqueror' became 'conqerer'. Every word had
a spelling mistake. I decided to investigate.*

A parent's enquiries may either lead to an investigation
by the school or they themselves may decide to learn
more about dyslexia to find ways to help their child.
If an older brother or sister had similar problems then
a parent may be quicker in suspecting that there is a
similar difficulty. It is also possible that, at this stage,
some parents may begin to question whether dyslexia
could explain some of their own difficulties.

At college or in the workplace

In further or higher education, about half the students who have dyslexic-type difficulties are either unaware of their dyslexia or do not mention it when they go into further or higher education. If they are lucky, a tutor may spot that they are having difficulties with written work and encourage them to seek advice.

It was OK at school. I just didn't take notes. I sometimes borrowed other people's and photocopied them. I mainly just read and re-read as much as I could of the textbooks we were given. When I got to college there was just too much reading to be able to do that and I started falling behind.

In the workplace, people sometimes discover that they may be dyslexic, or find their dyslexia is an issue when their role changes. They may have been promoted because they were good at their job and showed promise. They then find that their new job requires more literacy skills that give them some problems. This may lead their boss or line manager to suspect that the cause is dyslexia. Staff in human resources (personnel) departments are usually quite knowledgeable about a range of disabilities and difficulties these days – they have to be because of the Disability Discrimination Act 1995. They may suggest a work evaluation and a diagnostic assessment.

I suppose I had deliberately chosen work that allowed me to avoid too much reading and writing but actually I loved jewellery design and became very successful. The problems came when the company expanded and I was asked to take on some training that involved written materials. Then I panicked.

From a news item

Features and news items about dyslexia crop up frequently in the media, usually regarding 'cures' for dyslexia or new methods to teach children to read.

An article may report on an achievement by someone with dyslexia or a new piece of technology that could be useful. Most features include at least one account of someone's experience of struggling to read or failing at school, which may strike a chord and send you scurrying off for more information.

> *I saw this article about people who found the print was constantly moving on the page and I recognized the description immediately. It was me!*

'It all seems to add up'

Some dyslexic people have a very clear sense of the different way they respond to text, how they can never remember some words, how they feel confused by the letters. Some feel frustrated because they can't see their spelling mistakes. Others have vivid recollections of getting lost, trying to follow directions or instructions but always arriving late no matter how hard they tried. A non-dyslexic person may sympathize with such experiences and may experience them occasionally too. But another dyslexic person will recognize all these things: 'it all seems to add up.'

This personal account illustrates the sense of frustration an able person can feel:

> *He started explaining how to file documents on the computer. He 'double-clicked' and 'right-clicked' that and 'dragged' this and 'dropped' that. How could I know what was in which folder or document? More kept coming: jpeg, pdf, files, folders, back, forward, up, down . . . I felt more and more tearful and confused. Hopelessly, the tears of frustration streaked down my face as I tried to wrestle my*

*thoughts into the garble of words: 'You just have
to copy this to . . . Whenever you write this, just go
into . . .' The words ebbed and flowed ceaselessly.
Unless I pretended to agree, to nod wisely, to
indicate that I followed what he said – he would go
on trying so hard to explain things carefully and
simply. I could just about follow the words, but each
time he rephrased things to help me understand,
it felt like another set of information to grapple with.
I knew with a sinking feeling that I could not
remember any of it beyond the sound of his last
word.*

Three stories

Kamal at 26

When I was 21 I got my degree and began my training
as a primary school teacher. No one would have
believed that was possible when I was at school, least
of all me. My mum picked up on my struggles quickly
because my elder sister had had a dyslexia assessment
when she was 9. Although we tried really hard, no one
would help when I was 7, saying 'it was too early to be
sure' and it took nearly 3 years to get help in the
classroom for me. But this extra support made a
difference and I was lucky to get some more help
outside school and caught up even more. I wish we
hadn't had to wait so long because I was unhappy at
school for a long time and lost a lot of confidence.

Bill at 16

Bill experienced a lot of difficulty at school from the
start of his secondary years. The work that had been
more gently criticized before was now being sent back,
and the larger school with its corridors and different
places made it all even more confusing. To save face,
Bill began to misbehave – better to be thought of as
awkward rather than slow – especially with his peers.

In his GCSE year, one of his teachers suggested that he should be screened for dyslexia and this led to him being assessed. He got some extra help after school and began to make progress, especially in the subjects he liked. He found the use of a computer made a big difference in the work he could do and decided to go on into the sixth form. With extra time in examinations he was able to get into university, although he still tried to avoid too much reading.

Mary at 48

Mary had muddled through school never doing particularly well. Her talent in art and design led her to art college and she developed a career in fabric design. After several successful years, her firm wanted to promote her and urged her to take a qualification in business administration to help her in her new senior position. She began to panic, realizing that she found writing and organizing her paperwork very difficult. She sought study skills advice and it was then suggested that she might have dyslexia. Following her assessment she was offered help planning her studies and managed to complete the qualification.

Your own experience

In Activity 3 you can write your own story. Compare your story with those in the three stories above. Do you notice some similarities? You might have some unanswered questions. Be aware that dyslexia can overlap with other specific learning difficulties.

Other Specific Learning Difficulties (SpLD)

We haven't the space to discuss the range of specific learning difficulties. Some of these are closely related to dyslexia. Here is a summary of the terms you may come across. There is an overlap in the symptoms of all the

ACTIVITY 3
Writing about your own experiences

Now write your own story. This will help you to bring together all the information and experiences that may relate to your dyslexia. You can choose how you would like to do it:

- You can complete the sentences in the outline in Figure 2.2 or print out a copy from the website (printable document **17**) and add anything that you remember in the spaces provided.
- Cross out anything that doesn't apply to you.
- You can use the outline in Figure 2.2 to guide you and complete your story on a separate sheet.
- You can just let it flow onto paper in any order – forget the spelling etc.
- You could record it.

SpLDs so you may be dyslexic with some dyspraxic difficulties or you may have ADHD with some dyslexic-type difficulties. These are just labels. Sometimes labels can be helpful – in getting particular support for example. Sometimes they may be unhelpful. Use them only when you need or want to.

- **Dyspraxia** (also known as **DCD** – Developmental Co-ordination Disorder): literally means 'difficulty with doing'. It is an impairment of the brain cells responsible for the organization of movement (motor skills). This affects the planning of what to do and how to do it. Many people with dyslexia also have dyspraxia.

Figure 2.2 My story

This is an outline for you to add the details. Complete any relevant sentences. Add anything that you remember in the spaces provided and ask your family what they remember. Cross out anything that doesn't apply to you.

Before I went to school

I was a late talker. I found some words hard to say like __

_____

I was generally healthy/often poorly with _____

_____

_____

I had some hearing problems: _____

_____

I had some visual problems: _____

_____

I was clumsy with tying shoelaces, ball games and

_____

_____

My family

The language(s) spoken at home was (were)

_____

Other people in my family had difficulty with reading, spelling, writing, co-ordination, including [who?] _____

_____

Of these my [who?] _____
had a diagnosis of dyslexia.

Figure 2.2 My story – *continued*

At primary school

I remember being late learning to read. The words and letters seemed to _____

_____

I hated reading aloud because _____

_____

I found writing difficult because I am left-handed or because _____

_____

I had difficulty remembering the times tables _____

_____

The attitude of my teachers to my difficulties was _____

_____

I had extra help for _____

_____

I enjoyed primary school. I particularly liked _____

_____

I had a lot of time off school because _____

_____

At secondary school

My difficulties increased. In particular I found that _____

_____

Learning languages was difficult for me. I tried to learn [which one?] _____
but _____

_____

_____

Figure 2.2 My story – *continued*

I felt

    I worked hard ☐

    I was often behind ☐

    I used to bunk off school ☐

    I often switched off ☐

My teachers were

    supportive ☐   unaware ☐

    dismissive ☐   sarcastic ☐

    encouraging ☐   patient ☐

    indifferent ☐

I passed _____ O-levels / CSEs / GCSEs in [which subjects?] _____

_____

I passed _____ A-levels/Btec in [which subjects?] _____

_____

I left school aged _____

After school I did some more studying [what?]

_____

_____

My experience at college was

_____

_____

_____

_____

_____

_____

_____

_____

Figure 2.2 My story – *continued*

At work

My first job was _____

I enjoyed my work ☐   I hated my work ☐

I now work as _____

The attitude of my boss to my difficulties is _____
_____

I get help and support from colleagues _____
_____

I think I could progress further in my job if _____
_____

Me

The things I really find difficult include _____
_____

I try to avoid _____
_____

I have some good ways of getting round things such as
_____
_____

Things that I am good at include _____
_____
_____

I really enjoy _____
_____
_____

My most important aim in life is to _____
_____
_____

- **Dyscalculia:** means 'difficulty performing mathematical calculations'. It relates to difficulties relating to having a feel for size and quantity rather than not grasping mathematical concepts.
- **Attention Deficit Disorder (ADD):** is a medical condition that affects the ability to concentrate and maintain attention to tasks.
- **Attention Deficit Hyperactive Disorder (ADHD):** inattention combined with significantly heightened activity levels and impulsiveness.

Just be aware that a specific learning difficulty is independent of general ability (intelligence) but it can seriously get in the way of someone managing to do something that they would be expected to be capable of doing. It is therefore frustrating for that person as they have to devise or be helped to find ways around the problem, which will involve a lot of time and effort.

Taking time to assess yourself

There are many dyslexia checklists available. We have included one (Appendix A) but you may have already been through one from the British Dyslexia Association (BDA) or the Adult Dyslexia Organization (ADO). There are lots of checklists on the internet too. All these checklists are designed to help you decide whether you might be dyslexic. Some are more useful than others.

If you are reading this book because you think you might be dyslexic, now is the time to go through the checklist, add up the ticks and then think about what to do next. Here are a couple of options:

- Find a qualified assessor and discuss whether you need a full assessment (in Chapter 3 we discuss what this involves).
- Accept that you may be dyslexic and use this book for ideas to help you do those tasks that you have the most difficulty with.

There is no doubt that for some people the identification or diagnosis of dyslexia comes as a blessing. It is a relief to know you are not 'malingering' and that some of the comments you may have received in the past were indeed totally unfair.

It came as a huge relief to me – at last I knew I wasn't a fraud! I hadn't been lazy. Trying any harder wouldn't have worked.

 ACTIVITY 4
Identifying things to work on

- Jot down a few things you think your dyslexia makes more difficult.
- Assess how difficult: hard, very hard, impossible.
- Rank each item in order of how important it is for you to improve – with 1 being the most important.

You should end up with a list like the one in Figure 2.3.

Things I find difficult	How difficult	How important
Spelling	Very	1
Remembering names	Virtually impossible	3
Coping with so much reading	Hard	2

Figure 2.3 Identifying things to work on

In this chapter

In this chapter we have looked at:

- how you might feel about dyslexia;
- how you found out about your dyslexia;
- how it affects you;
- what you'd like to work on to improve.

We hope we have encouraged you to think. Mull it all over before you read on. You don't have to progress by taking each chapter in order. If something has triggered your curiosity in another chapter, that's fine – do it your way.

Make this book work for you!

3

How dyslexia affects you

In this chapter we help you to find out how you work best, what your strengths are and how you can use your dyslexia assessment report if you have one.

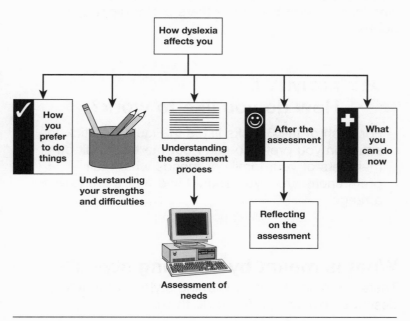

Figure 3.1 Summary of Chapter 3

How you prefer to do things

We all have different ways of working. Here are a few:

- on our own
- in groups
- at home
- in a reference library
- sitting at a desk
- sitting in an armchair
- on the train
- on the beach

Which one suits you best?

Some people like to work through structured courses with lessons and tutors or others prefer dipping into books.

 ACTIVITY 5
How do you like to work?

For each of the 3 tasks listed in Figure 3.2, tick the situation you prefer to carry out the task. Ask other members of your family or friends what their preferences are – you should find that there is quite a range.

What is meant by 'learning styles'?

There are many kinds of learning styles but they all describe how you prefer to do things.

Sensory learning style

We learn by using our senses:

- seeing;
- hearing; and
- doing (which also includes smelling and touching).

	Tasks		
	Reading a report or proposal	Writing a letter or essay	Learning how to use a piece of equipment
In a small group of people			
Sitting at a table			
In an armchair or deckchair			
In a quiet place			
With background music			
Other (specify)			

Figure 3.2 For use with Activity 5

Many people use these senses equally and often together. These people are 'multi-sensory' learners. Some people use one or two senses more than the others. Using more than one sense improves learning.

Have you thought about the way you prefer to learn?

 ACTIVITY 6
Sensory learning style

 There is a *Learning style questionnaire* that you can print out from our online resource, printable document **2**. You can also find out from there how to interpret your results. Try the questions now. Your answers will tell you more about the way you prefer to do things.

By now you should be able to identify some of your strengths – which sense or senses you use best for a particular task.

The cognitive learning style

It's useful to think about what is called your 'cognitive' learning style. This is about the *ways* you think and deal with information. By considering these you are identifying some more of your strengths.

There are four main cognitive styles shown in Figure 3.3.

When looking at our cognitive learning style we consider two things:
- how we think; and
- how we take in and process information.

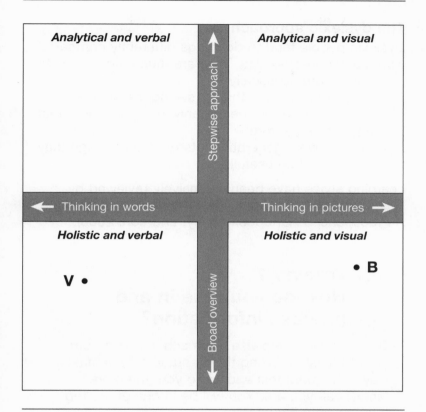

Figure 3.3 Cognitive learning styles
(**V** and **B** = the authors' positions)

How do you think?

- Do you think in words or in images such as pictures, diagrams?
- If you think in words you'll be in one of the two left-hand boxes.
- If you think in images, you'll be in one of the two right-hand boxes.
- The more you think in words, the more you are a 'verbalizer'.
- The more you think in pictures, the more you are 'visual'.

The dyslexic approach

Dyslexic people tend to do things differently compared with many non-dyslexics. They are much more likely to:

- think more holistically;
- be more intuitive – that is, seeing the answer to something but not necessarily knowing where that answer came from;
- be creative – generating lots of ideas, though they may not all be useful!

Learning styles have been extensively reviewed by Tilly Mortimer in her book: *Dyslexia and Learning Style: A Practitioner's Handbook* (Wiley, 2nd edn, 2008).

 ACTIVITY 7
How do you take in and process information?

Do you take a stepwise approach, reading from start to finish, thinking things out in a systematic way? The more this applies to you, the more 'analytical' you are. You will be in one of the top two boxes in Figure 3.3.

Do you take a broad overview, an intuitive approach, see things as a whole? The more this applies to you, the more 'holistic' you are. You will fall into one of the bottom two boxes. So which box do you fall in for both thinking and processing?

We did this exercise: Vicki (V) is holistic and verbal, Bonita (B) is holistic and visual.

Figure 3.4 gives you some general ideas and approaches to try for each of the four cognitive styles. These ideas and more are discussed in Chapters 5 to 10.

Analytical and verbal	Analytical and visual
Try: • tape recorders • checklists • mnemonics • chanting and singing • making notes • looking for key words	Try: • visual images • videos • flow charts • wall planners • using colour • talking books • diagrams
Holistic and verbal	**Holistic and visual**
Try: • walking about when thinking • speaking ideas onto tape • dictating to someone who can sort your ideas for you • making notes • familiarization • looking for key words	Try: • mind maps • posters • drawings • diagrams • 3-dimensional models • using colour • familiarization • talking books

Figure 3.4 Ideas to try

Understanding *your* strengths and difficulties

Metacognition – understanding how you learn

The word 'metacognition' just means being aware of the way you learn and do things! By now you should be getting a better idea. You are developing metacognitive skills (meta-cog-nitive: *meta* is Greek for 'among, with, beside, after', and *cognitio* is Latin for 'getting to know').

Metacognitive skills enable us to know how we think and the processes involved in thinking. Being aware of the way you think is extremely useful when it comes to choosing strategies. The dyslexia assessment process can help to identify your skills and strengths.

- *I can never understand a recipe until I have made it.*
- *Please don't give me verbal directions. I'm better with a map – I think in pictures.*
- *When I meet someone new I have to call them by their name at least three times to be able to remember it.*

Understanding the assessment process

If you are dyslexic, you may have been assessed more than once:

- as a child at school;
- again at school for exam 'concessions' or 'accommodations' – we prefer the term 'exam facilities';
- at college, university or work.

You may only have been 'screened' for dyslexia – taking some short basic tests to identify the possibility of dyslexia. In adults, dyslexia can be difficult to detect because they seem to be coping. Your reading and writing attainment may be at a similar level to that expected from your ability but this conceals the difficulties you have and the time it takes to complete work. People in this situation are often called 'compensated dyslexics' because they have found ways around many of the difficulties. It is still worth having an assessment.

If you have been assessed then Activity 8 is designed to help you think about the process. If you have never been assessed and want to know more about the screening and assessment processes and tests, go to the *General* section of our online resources.

✏️ ACTIVITY 8
How you were assessed

Here are some questions about how you were assessed. Tick the answers that are closest to yours.

- How many times have you had some form of assessment for dyslexia or 'specific learning difficulties'?
  several times ☐   once ☐   never ☐

- Were you (or your family) given a copy of the report?
  yes ☐   no ☐   not sure ☐

- Did the assessors go through it with you or your family?
  yes ☐   no ☐   not sure ☐

- Did you read it at the time or later?
  at the time ☐   later ☐   never ☐

- Did you understand it?
  yes ☐   no ☐   not sure ☐

Being assessed

If you have been assessed, take a moment to assess the assessment. Answer the questions below and read our comments. If you haven't been assessed yet or you're going to be reassessed, you can still look at the comments and use them to ask your assessor to explain the processes. An assessment will include tests, observations and an interview.

- *Can you remember how long your assessment took?*
  A full assessment can be a positive and illuminating experience, although it can take 3 hours or more and involves a lot of concentration.
- *Can you remember what you discovered from the experience?*
  Many of the things you are asked to do are things that have given you difficulties for most of your life. It can be a very emotional and exhausting experience.
- *Were the tests explained to you? Were you given an idea of what the tests were revealing as you worked through them?*

  There are some explanations in the *General* section of our online resource.
- *Was the attitude of the assessor friendly and positive? If you were assessed as an adult, did the assessor understand your needs as an adult?*
  There are fewer assessors with experience of adults. When the results of tests in the report are quoted in children's ages, this can feel insulting. However, attitudes have changed and more tests specifically for adults are now available.
- *Did the experience touch on bad memories?*
  This is understandable. Many of you will have had bad experiences at school: working hard but seeming to get nowhere, being told you were lazy or stupid, losing interest in lessons, even playing truant. Adults often ask why their dyslexia was not identified before and feel angry because of this.
- *Was the report clear and comprehensible to you?*
  Many reports are written in technical language – ask for explanations.

- *Did you have the opportunity to discuss the report with the assessor or with someone else?*
  If possible, contact the assessor again and ask them to explain the findings in straightforward language. Otherwise, a specialist teacher may be able to help. The report is, after all, about *you* – and should be *for* you too.

Whatever your assessment experience was, now is the time to concentrate on moving forward.

Needs assessments

A needs assessor will be looking at how your particular difficulties can be best supported by technology (high, medium and low) and by people such as specialist tutors. Such an assessment is required if you wish to apply for disabled student allowances (DSAs), which are available to students in higher education to pay for equipment and support. Dyslexia is deemed to be a disability under the Disability Discrimination Act 1995. If you are in work, you may have a technical assessment through the Access to Work scheme. Both are funded or part-funded by the government. In Chapters 5 to 10 you will find ideas that you can discuss with a needs assessor.

After the assessment

Pause for a moment

Well, how closely *did* you look at your dyslexia report when you first saw it?

Do you ever go back to look at it? If so, for what reason?

ACTIVITY 9
Reflecting on the assessment

Why not take another look at your assessment report and try the activity in the *General* section of our online resource, *assessment report activity*.

You may find it really useful to do this with someone else, e.g. a teacher, tutor or line manager.

What you can do now

1 At the start of this chapter we looked at your approaches to learning and working, and how you use your senses (Activities 5 and 6).

You can keep a record of your strengths and how you use them in a file that you can call your 'toolbox of strategies and ideas'.

Keep a note of how you do things. Note ways that are particularly successful. You could jot down something like this:

- Use large sticky notes on car dashboard with directions.
- Spelling strategy: break down a word into two – 'con-science'.

2 Look (again) at the recommendations in your dyslexia report. Which ones have you done something about?

Sometimes adult reading can be improved by 'reading programmes' and you may like to try one with a specialist tutor. Some adults prefer to develop other strategies.

Are there recommendations that might be worth thinking about again? Part 2 of this book can help you with ideas.

How did you feel when you were assessed?

Think about this example:

*He ran up the stairs to his bedroom shouting angrily:
'I won't be dyslexic, I won't!'*

*His elder brother, also dyslexic, said reassuringly: 'It's
good to know! I was really pleased when they told
me because they would know it wasn't all my fault.
You will be able to get extra help and they won't yell
at you for being careless.'*

Reactions to the assessment are very varied – here are a
few:

Relief	Tearful	Angry
Disbelief	Horror	Excited
Panic	Unhappy	Depressed
Positive	Delighted	Frustrated
Thrilled	Inspired	Emotional

Circle the ones that relate to you.

You have probably experienced all these feelings and
more at some time or another. And this is
understandable. Different stages in your life will produce
different reactions. How did you cope, or how are you
coping with all these emotions?

Many people who were assessed as adults will need to
talk things over with someone. The person who
assessed you may have helped you work through your
feelings and explained to you what it all means. You may
still want to talk to someone.

If you were assessed as a child, the talking may have
been with your parents rather than with you. You may
find that you need to talk to someone now you are an
adult. Here is a selection of feelings from people who
had just been assessed:

It was such a relief that I burst into tears. All of a sudden I realized that I wasn't thick, stupid or lazy. I was me – creative but with some difficulties.

Depression hit me – I couldn't talk about it for weeks. Then at a meeting someone told me that I was a great lateral thinker!

It was when I started my new job that it hit me. I found myself really angry because there were so many things to cope with.

I was staggered! But then I started to feel very positive – this will be a real challenge.

Which of these is you?

- ☺ You have known about your dyslexia for a long time and are comfortable with it.
- ☺ You have known about your dyslexia for a long time and are still coming to terms with it.
- ☺ You have suspected that you are dyslexic for a long time but still haven't been formally diagnosed.
- ☺ You learned about it very recently and are greatly relieved.
- ☹ You learned about it very recently and are concerned about what it might mean.

It is perfectly understandable for people to have some uncomfortable feelings about their dyslexia. The reasons for this are probably related to the way the world perceives dyslexia. Changing attitudes to dyslexia are referred to in Chapter 4.

Postscript

You are the most important person to consider your needs. You know yourself better than anyone else does. The actress Susan Hampshire once wrote:

> *One of the worst aspects of being dyslexic is the vicious circle caused by stress. As soon as I make a mistake I panic, and because I panic I make more mistakes.*

Throughout this book you will find ideas for coping strategies that will help to reduce stress.

You can find some specific suggestions for stress management and relaxation techniques in the *General* section of our online resource. Improving self-esteem also helps – see Chapter 8.

In this chapter

If you have worked your way through this chapter and the two previous ones, you should be beginning to understand:

- your own particular variety of dyslexia;
- your cognitive style;
- the way you learn;
- your strengths and your weaknesses.

You should also be beginning to discover what you need to do the things you want to do. Part 2 of this book will help you identify ideas and strategies that you can use.

4

Support from those close to you

This chapter looks at how the attitudes of family and friends can help and how those close to you can be involved in giving support and encouragement.

> Most importantly
> I knew they
> believed in me and
> would back me all
> the way

> She always found
> time to read stuff
> through for me
> whenever I
> wanted

If your family or friends know very little about dyslexia it would be a good idea for them to read the section below, where we talk briefly about how attitudes to dyslexia have changed over the years. They will be in a better position to back you up when they know more about the issues that affect you. They can also help to update those who still think dyslexia is just about reading!

Changing attitudes to dyslexia

Word blindness

In the 19th century, as more and more people received an education of sorts, some people had an unexpected difficulty with reading. This difficulty was put down to 'word blindness' and the term persisted until well into the 20th century. Only a very few got any help. Some drifted into the more practical trades and professions and often excelled.

'It must be your fault'

When individuals could not learn to read or write for no obvious reason, they were all too often seen as being to blame. They were called slow, thick, lazy or ineducable. Some of them who came from more privileged backgrounds might have been lucky enough to find a good and sensitive teacher who, by trying all sorts of teaching methods, would have hit on a multi-sensory approach and managed to help them make some progress. These teachers realized something else was going on but couldn't identify what it was. They called it word blindness.

Damaged centres in the brain

In the early 20th century scientists studying the brain realized that the things we do seem to relate to specific centres of the brain. This was a rather simplified approach but it laid the foundations for modern neurology – the science of the brain and nervous system. People researching dyslexia suggested that it was related to some of these centres being impaired.

Some brains don't work the same way

It was when doctors were investigating spoken and written language deficits in stroke patients that the first neurological research was carried out. It showed damage in the left hemisphere of the brain, which was later to be identified as a main control area for language. This kind of dyslexia is called 'acquired' dyslexia. It was through examining such brains that further research revealed the different ways the brain used and handled data (see Chapter 1). At the same time the pioneering work of Samuel Orton in the US suggested that dyslexia is due to abnormal development in children and coined the term 'developmental dyslexia' to cover the much more common occurrence. Orton believed that remediation was entirely possible so some enlightened schools and teachers began using remediation programmes.

Some brains work differently

Further understanding of the brain using the relatively recent and expensive brain scanning equipment has led to the neurological differences being established beyond all doubt. The causes of dyslexic difficulties are not fully understood but weak phonological processing (problems with recognizing sounds and linking them to letters), short-term memory problems and different neurological processing, are generally acknowledged as key factors.

In the 21st century

Dyslexia is now well recognized and accepted throughout the world, but there are still people whose understanding of it is not up to date. Teacher training courses spend insufficient time on how to teach reading and resources are always stretched. Following the Rose report of 2009, more money has been put into teacher training and specialist professional development.

The awareness of dyslexia in the general population comes mainly from TV and radio programmes, or articles in the press. People may be aware of the dyslexic difficulties associated with reading, writing and spelling, but they may not know about problems with memory and organization. We have suggested some ways to cope in every chapter of this book.

Possible roles for family and friends

The attitudes of, and support from, the people around you are important to your success. Above all it is important that they are encouraging and positive, that they see you as a person with skills, abilities and needs, and focus on your strengths. Talking to them about the things that you find hard and the ways you find it easier to do things is really good. Even those very close to you cannot necessarily see how it feels for you. Moreover, some other family members may have mixed feelings because of their own similar difficulties.

Sometimes talking with a counsellor (see the end of Chapter 8, Self-esteem and motivation) can be really helpful in learning how to handle stress and the confusion that you may feel at different stages in your life. It can also be really useful for you in clarifying what you want to change and why.

How a partner can help you

Can we change how we do things – will others let us? A partner can get into the habit of doing something for you instead of you finding out how to help yourself. Sometimes they are just not sure how to help you. It can be helpful if you can explain what help and support would be useful. Phrases such as:

- Can you show me slowly how to do that?
- Please keep encouraging me – it really helps.
- It would really help if you . . .

How family and friends can help you at work or in education

Family and friends can help you to trust your own competence. They can help and encourage you to seek feedback from teachers or colleagues. If you have never been assessed, they can encourage you to have an assessment, particularly if you are going on to further or higher education. Many dyslexic people may manage at school but only start to find some difficulties insurmountable when facing the challenges of advanced education or advancement in their career. It is then that they can find help from family and friends incredibly reassuring and practical too (see below).

How you can get teachers to help you with feedback

We are all more likely to increase our efforts if we are encouraged and given positive appraisal. So, ask your teachers for constructive feedback so that you can decide whether to alter the original goal or, perhaps, adjust your expectations. This may mean that you decide you need more training or more time to reach the goal. If they ask you what they can do to help, ask them to help you monitor your progress. Looking back over this reveals just how much progress you have made.

How a parent can help a learner still at school

It is impossible to overstate the importance of the early years in helping every child to develop confidence in themselves and their potential. It is much easier to build up a child's self-esteem than to help them recover from low self-esteem later on; self-esteem developed in childhood is longer lasting and more resilient. Parents can help and encourage their child to see that reading and writing skills are separate from understanding the content. They can help ensure that teachers are informed and encouraged to be helpful. Their belief in their child as a wonderful and worthwhile human being is vital.

Because difficulties can increase over time, parents should not wait to see if their child 'grows out of it'. They must listen to what the child is saying about their difficulties and clarify with their child what the cause

| **Having positive attitudes** |
| Family and friends can: |
| be accepting of your individuality |
| get an understanding of what dyslexia is |
| ask *you* what they can do to help – rather than making assumptions about what would be useful for you |
| give you lots of encouragement to keep you going – praise and encouragement raises the spirit |
| concentrate on your strengths – remind you of past successes |
| |
| |
| |

| **Giving practical help** |
| Family and friends can: |
| take on some home tasks at really busy times to relieve you of pressure |
| build in some stress-release activities |
| help your reading fluency through paired reading (see Chapter 5) |
| let you use their computer or help you with yours; record material for you to play on your iPod |
| help with checking your work |
| rewrite or reword instructions – often these are badly written |
| help with costs of assessment, equipment, books, tutoring etc.; gifts of money also act as encouragement |
| |
| |
| |

Figure 4.1 Family and friends

might be. This may need the help of a professional with experience in dyslexia. So:

- follow up difficulties with literacy – get help, don't be put off;
- help with their school work when you can.

Make contact with the teachers so that the help given at school and at home is complementary.

Finally, helpful things your family and friends can do

There are some really helpful things that those who know you well can do. We have made two lists. There's space to add your own ideas too. See Figure 4.1.

In this chapter

You should now realize that attitudes have changed and are still changing. By understanding more about dyslexia you are in a position to explain what it is and so help others to understand it better.

PART 2

Finding the best way for you

There are 6 chapters in this section. Each one takes a different aspect of everyday tasks and suggests strategies you might like to try. Most of these strategies have been creatively devised by or with dyslexic people in various situations. You don't have to try everything at once.

- Chapter 5
  Reading and the world of print
  Reading strategies and activities

- Chapter 6
  Getting down what you want to say
  Writing strategies and activities for a range of situations

- Chapter 7
  Getting done what you want to do
  Strategies and activities for planning and organization

- Chapter 8
  Self-esteem and motivation
  Understanding self-esteem and improving your confidence

- Chapter 9
  Handling numbers
  Strategies and activities based around dealing with numbers

- Chapter 10
  Making memory work for you
  Developing strategies for remembering

You may want to dip into the area that gives you the most problems. That's fine – but there are ideas in some chapters that can be adapted for other areas. Use these ideas to devise your own strategies because your own ideas will work best for you.

5

Reading and the world of print

Was dyslexia ever a problem before the invention of the printing press?

In this chapter we look at:

- how we got into the business of reading;
- what is involved in the process and what skills are required;
- deciding what you want to read;
- reading strategies;
- improving comprehension;
- help available.

How reading became important

Today we seem to rely on print for much of our information, whether on paper or on screen. We seem to have forgotten that for many years, people managed without it – but that doesn't mean there were no complicated ideas or concepts. People relied on speech and oral traditions to exchange information and ideas. Migrants and travelling storytellers passed them on. Human brains, it seems, are geared up biologically for

speech but not for the entirely separate and difficult business of reading and writing. Although writing had been around for a very long time, before the arrival of the printing press, intelligent and articulate people traded, invented and communicated – but mostly by word of mouth. Some people used scribes to write important letters. Writers, usually priests, were specialists. In the same way today, government ministers employ speech writers and reports are written by civil servants. Even public examinations were conducted verbally at Oxford and Cambridge universities – there were no written examinations until the middle of the 17th century.

The invention of the printing press rapidly increased the availability of printed materials, so literacy became a skill needed by more and more people. Acquiring knowledge and information became more closely linked with the skill of reading – decoding print. Then the printing press made words on paper accessible to many more people. Mass education in the developing countries used oral teaching and learning ('rote' learning) until well into the 20th century. There was little understanding about the nature of literacy skills.

Now, in the 21st century, print dominates our education and our access to knowledge and information. Our ability is too often measured by how good we are at reading and writing. Our qualifications are mainly gained by written exams. However, another communication revolution as great as, or greater than that of the invention of the printing press, has taken place with the introduction of computer technology. We can change the format (the print, the layout, the colour etc.) of the text, and the technology can even read it back to us. We can click and copy and paste, and we can use icons. Producing written materials using technology is changing the way we look at reading and writing skills.

How we read

So what exactly is going on when we are reading? Have a look again at Chapter 1, which explains the process of how we read in some detail. Figure 5.1 gives a brief summary of how our brains work in reading. If you find this particularly interesting and want to know how we *learn* to read, please refer to the additional information (mentioned in Chapter 1) in the *Reading* section of our online resource.

Most dyslexic people have phonological difficulties so they rely more on the visual route. You can recognize a word from visual cues independent of sound. You can recognize lots of words from your internal store and so

Brain working **visually**	Brain working **phonologically**
We recognize familiar and short words visually – the shape of the word and the letters.	By recognizing letters and groups of letters, knowing the sounds and putting them together.
Examples • the • of, off • that, than	**Examples** • b – a – tch

Pitfalls
But we can confuse these and get them wrong
 	
    'I miss out the little words – I just don't see them'
 	
Missing out 'not' can change the meaning completely!
	Pitfalls
	But some letter combinations are difficult to learn because they have many different sounds or don't sound at all.
	
	    'the ph *in physics always threw me'*

Figure 5.1 How the brain works when reading

can read them rapidly. For example, you can probably recognize the word 'dyslexia' just by looking at it but you may have to sound out 'cholesterol', 'herbaceous' or 'physical' to recognize them.

There are other kinds of pitfalls. If you find it difficult to recognize letters or words, it can really slow you down:

- getting the letter wrong – confusing 'b' and 'd' for example;
- mistaking 'of' for 'off' or 'in' for 'on';
- missing out words or parts of words;

- getting the wrong sound for a letter or group of letters.

But there are some good clues to help you read. For example:

He scored a g _ _ _ .

You don't need the other letters to guess the rest of the word correctly because you can get it from the context.

You are also using your knowledge of the *meaning* of words (semantics). For example:

The museum visited the boy *or*
The boy visited the museum.

It is very clear from the meaning of the words which sentence is correct.

The fact that letters are grouped into words helps us to read. Without this grouping of letters, reading becomes more difficult.

Now try the following sentence:

On ceup on atim ether ewereth reebe ars

Could you decode that? (Answer at the bottom of the page.) The different grouping of the letters means you have to spend much more energy processing the information – and less time understanding. Because handwriting is more variable in shape and size, these problems are more likely to occur when reading handwritten work.

We have a tendency to skim over familiar words.

Finished files are the result of many years of study.

How many f's are there in that sentence? Many people only see 2 at first. They miss the 'f' in the word 'of' because they skim over it.

Answer: Once upon a time there were three bears

Pause for a moment

What can you do about your reading as an adult? Here are two possibilities:

- work on improving your phonological skills;
- build and extend your visual vocabulary.

There are many tutors, teachers as well as resources on the internet to help you improve your decoding skills and reading rate, which are worth exploring. This may take a lot of time but can make a big difference. It will also help you to work on some of the useful strategies we describe below. What you choose to work on all depends on what you want to do at the time.

We tend to read important things more carefully:

> *I read novels just following the names of the main characters and leaving out all the descriptive stuff. I couldn't read my student books like that because I had to remember and understand it all in a much more critical way.*

Before you look at the strategy ideas further on, it is worth deciding what it is you would really like to read. Then you can choose the right strategy for you for that kind of reading. You will probably end up with several strategies for different types of reading. This is called 'flexible reading' and most successful readers do it all the time. Whether you are reading study books, instructions, a report, a book about your hobby, a novel, a newspaper, you still need strategies to help make sense of the texts.

As we have said, there are many types of reading matter. We will be suggesting a number of strategies to help you improve your reading, your concentration and your comprehension. The table in Figure 5.3 summarizes the strategies that you could try for different reading tasks. You will also need to decide whether you should read something in detail or read it at all! Our *'Do I need to read this?*' strategy can help you decide. You can find this in the *Reading* section of our online resource.

You may find other strategies that are helpful – add them to the table in Figure 5.3 for future reference.

It isn't necessary to read every word, every paragraph, chapter or section – you can just read what you need for that particular occasion.

 ACTIVITY 10
What kind of reading do you do?

Find two different things you have read today such as:
- a form
- an article in a newspaper or magazine
- a book
- some instructions.

Use Figure 5.2 to think about each one in more detail. Ask yourself the questions; you might like to jot down the answers. For a blank copy refer to printable document **10** on our online resource.

Look at your answers. Are they roughly similar for each item or do you find some things easier?

Which difficulties frustrate you the most? Mark these with a star as they might be worth working on.

Hopefully this gives you a better idea of what reading is like for you and where you think some strategies might be useful.

		Item you read:	
		Report of football match	
1	Did you read all the words?		*No*	
2	Did you hear them in your head as you read them?		*No*	
3	Did you find there were some words which you guessed the meaning from the rest of the sentence?		*Yes – several*	
4	Did you get lost on long sentences?		*No long sentences*	
5	Did you have to reread any of them to make sure you understood what it was about?		*Yes*	
6	Did you take any breaks from reading?		*Not a long report*	
7	How long did you read before feeling you had read enough or couldn't take in any more?		*5 min*	

Figure 5.2 For use with Activity 10

Type of reading materials	Suggested strategies explained in detail below this figure
Notices	• Read the key words • Make notes • Electronic dictionary or reading pen
Instructions	• Make them visual • Record them
Newspapers	• Read headlines only • Listen to radio or TV as alternative source of news • Or use news online with a screen reader
Reports	• Read and record, then listen • Have document in digital format • Make notes – helps you to focus • See online resource
Magazines/ journals	• Talking books • Read-out computer facility
Letters	• Encourage people to type – easier to read • Or email
Text and reference books	• Read-out computer facility • Record complex passages • Make notes – helps you to focus
Novels (fiction)	• Talking books • Videos • Choose the right level – see handout: 'Reading levels'

Figure 5.3 Summary of strategies to use

Assessing what you need to read and what you can leave out

If you have to read quite a lot of material – you may be:

- a student;
- writing a report for work;
- working on a project;
- writing an article for a magazine.

In addition, you are likely to have to be selective in what you read.

If you are faced with too much reading you can sort things into:

- essential;
- desirable;
- non-essential.

 You could ask someone at work or college to give you some pointers or assistance. You can find some help in the additional information *Do I need to read this?* in the *Reading* section of our online resources.

Your toolbox: for reading

This section contains some ideas that may help improve your reading skills. These are summarized in Figure 5.4.

The print

A variety of different styles of print – called 'fonts' – are used for printing material:

Arial looks like this.

This is Times New Roman

Flemish script is hard to read

Comic Sans doesn't have serifs.

Size can be varied and is measured in 'points'. All the above are in 12 point! Try out some of these variations on your word processor. Which do you find best to read?

◇ Toolbox: Strategies for reading

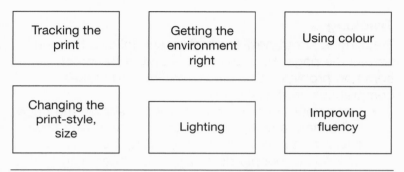

| Tracking the print | Getting the environment right | Using colour |

| Changing the print-style, size | Lighting | Improving fluency |

Figure 5.4 Ideas in the reading strategies toolbox

Most dyslexic readers prefer fonts that are simple, without serifs (the curly bits) and a point size of about 12. It is easier for most people to read text that is only justified (lined up) on the left hand side. You may find that you avoid reading certain items because the print is so unfriendly, for example when text is printed over photographs. Some of the strategies in this 'toolbox' will help to make reading easier on the eye.

In summary, unlike the print in books and journals, you have control of the material you generate on your computer and you can ask others to help you by printing out material for you:

- on the paper of your preferred colour;
- using your preferred font;
- in your preferred point size;
- left justified only.

Alternatively, they could give you the text electronically so that you can change it to your own specific preferences. If you have the technology, you can scan in text and then reformat it to suit you – see Chapter 11.

Otherwise, if point size is a problem for some essential reading, you could try enlarging (or reducing) it to suit you.

Tracking

Tracking is about how easily your eye follows the print across the page. Poor tracking is one of the most common problems that slows reading and makes comprehension difficult. Try:

- using your finger to trace the word across the page – this has recently been suggested as a way for everyone to speed up their reading. You will see all kinds of people doing this – it's becoming fashionable!
- using a ruler or a piece of card – not under the line you are reading but above. This will allow your eye to read on but doesn't allow it to drift back.

People can learn to read a little quicker, sometimes a lot quicker. Furthermore, Tony Buzan, author of many books on study skills, states that this is possible for dyslexic people too. He suggests we have to:

- push on across the page;
- and never go back.

To help increase your reading rate, try the ideas on tracking suggested above.

Lighting

The best light to read under is daylight (but not direct sunlight), so ideally you need to sit near the window. The light should fall over the left shoulder (or the right shoulder, if you are writing and are left-handed) but avoid shadow or glare. If you are using a desk-lamp make sure it is in the right position so that the light falls on the page but doesn't cause reflections or glare. The lamp shouldn't be the only source of light in the room because too much contrast doesn't help.

Colour

Colour and lighting can make a huge difference to your reading rate and comfort. The high contrast between very white paper and black print can cause distortions and discomfort for many people. If you have trouble with reading, it may be because of visual discomfort and distortion of print on the page. A white page may seem to 'glare'. You may have a feeling of eye strain or even get headaches when you read. Words may appear to move, jumble or blur. Shadows may seem to fall on the page. All this interferes with reading, and reduces attention and concentration. For examples of what print can look like see Figure 1.5 in Chapter 1.

You can experiment with:
- using a highlighter pen to colour sections of text that you are finding difficult to read or understand. It isn't a crime to mark your own book and it can be very useful for visual clues;
- coloured overlays or tinted lenses;
- different lighting conditions – type of bulb, direction of light, position of lamp or lamps (see Chapter 11).

The section about *visual discomfort* (in the *Reading* section of our online resource) includes more information and a couple of things you can try to check whether coloured overlays might be helpful.

Getting your environment right

Sitting position. Ideally for reading you need to sit fairly upright so that you are not putting pressure on your spine but on your 'sitting' bones. Sitting more upright also means a better supply of air and blood to the brain and more brain power. Your reading distance should be about 50 cm (20 in) away from your eyes to give maximum peripheral and central vision. Sitting properly, ensuring that the temperature is comfortable and that your clothes are not tight will all enhance your reading stamina.

Distractions

Absolute silence is not always the best when you are reading. You need to avoid being interrupted, but music in the background can be beneficial to concentration so experiment with this where possible.

Improving your fluency

There are two good ways of improving your fluency in reading. One, called 'paired reading', is a great way for a friend or relative to help you. Paired reading:

- involves reading aloud with someone who is a fluent reader;
- helps you to become a more fluent reader.

You read in turns and get help when you need it. Guidance on *paired reading* can be found in the *Reading* section of our online resource.

The other useful method is to read at the right level for you. Choose a text with shorter sentences and very few unfamiliar words. You can work at reading a little faster if you use a slightly easier level.

Alternatively you could try the 'Simplified Measure of Gobbledygook' (SMOG) method of working out the readability. This is explained in the *Reading* section of our online resource.

The easiest way to work out the readability level of a text is to use an online SMOG calculator. In Spring 2009, NIACE made a new calculator available on its website at

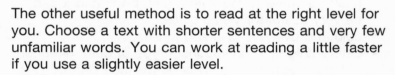

> www.niace.org.uk/misc/SMOG-calculator/
> smogcalc.php#

Skimming and scanning

Skimming is different from reading quickly. It is a way of getting the general gist (idea) of something by picking out key words and ideas that catch your eye as you

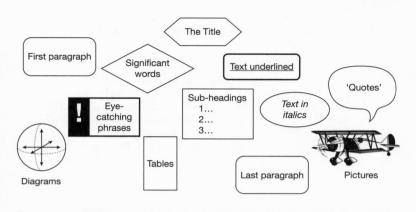

Figure 5.5 Things to look for when skimming

skim over the page. Many dyslexic people claim it is impossible for them while others are extremely good doing this. It uses holistic strengths, i.e. getting an overall picture from various bits of information.

You don't have to start at the beginning either – you can let your eye jump about, taking in those pieces of information you are drawn to – see Figure 5.5. You get an overall impression of what it's all about.

It's like looking at the paintings of Impressionists such as Cezanne – you know what the painting is about but you don't need to look at the detail to enjoy it.

Scanning, on the other hand, is a process of looking over some text to find a particular piece of information. You may, for example, scan something you've read in detail before going back to look for something you remember reading, such as a name or date.

◇ **Toolbox: Strategies for comprehension**

Being active: engage with what you are reading	Making notes	Making your personal dictionary
	Getting familiar with the topic	Reading in chunks and taking breaks

Figure 5.6 Ideas in the comprehension strategies toolbox

Your toolbox for comprehension

In this section we give you some ideas to help with your comprehension, i.e. understanding and remembering what you read. These are summarized in Figure 5.6.

If a lot of your energy goes into working out the words, then it can be hard to follow the line of thought through the sentence.

◇ Make your reading active

Being an *active* reader helps you to understand what you are reading better. This also helps you to remember what you've read. Ways of being a more active reader include:

Speaking a summary:

- Try reading a piece of text then, without looking at it, sum it up in your own words, recording what you say.
- Listen to what you have said with the text in front of you.

Highlighting:

- As you read, underline in pencil the bits you think are important. Then choose some of these to highlight in colour.
- Put a mark in the margin to indicate something important.

Ask questions as you read:

- What does the author want me to get out of this?
- Where is the author coming from – do they have a vested interest?
- How is it relevant to what I want?

And to help remember what you've read:

- Tell someone about what you have read and discuss it with them.
- Act it out.
- Use the SQ3R method (see the *Reading* section of our online resource):
    - Scan
    - Question
    - Read
    Remember
    Review.

Making some short notes:

- Try making short notes in your own words at the end of each paragraph as you read – see below.

◇ Making notes

Note making is a helpful strategy. It makes your reading active and you can keep the notes as a permanent record if necessary. Making notes:
- helps you concentrate;
- aids your understanding of what you are reading by putting it in your own words;
- helps you to organize your thinking;
- helps you to identify the main points;

- helps you to remember what you have read;
- gives you something to refer back to that is shorter and more concise.

You can find ideas of ways to make notes in Chapter 6 (*note making* section).

How to practise making notes:
- Choose a general, easy text to practise on.
- Identify the main issues and any new vocabulary.
- Try making a mind-map or diagram – see Chapter 6 (section on *making a plan*).

◇ Approaching a new topic

It is a lot easier to read about a subject that you are familiar with. If you want to learn more about a new topic try to find a children's book on the subject – a basic book, some introductory information on the internet, in a magazine or encyclopaedia. Children's books, like those published by Usborne for example, are particularly useful because they are written for less experienced readers – information is often expressed in simpler sentences and well-chosen vocabulary. This makes it easier to cope with new words. Once the new vocabulary becomes more familiar and the basic ideas are clearer, you can move on to a more detailed text. Many children's texts are simply better written because they have fewer unnecessary words. Long complex sentences add nothing to meaning but make it harder for dyslexic readers.

◇ Personal dictionary

Keep a note of new words that you want to remember. Using an address book is particularly helpful as you can keep the words in alphabetical order. You could include:
- useful words that you tend to stumble over or forget the meaning of;
- words you have difficulty spelling;

- words that you have to use in your work, your hobbies, your studies.

You can also use it for names of people you need to remember.

You can find some examples in the *Spelling* section of our online resource.

◇ Chunking

Read in meaningful chunks. You can, for example, read everything under one sub-heading and take a break before going on to the next.
- Read the title, headings and first and last paragraphs or sections to get an overview.
- Read a paragraph at a time, pause after each and ask yourself – what was that mainly about?
- Take regular breaks.

◇ Using time and taking breaks

On average, we cannot maintain a high level of concentration for more than about 20 minutes. So, if you are reading something that is quite demanding, make sure you take regular breaks.

ACTIVITY 11
Reading times

Try reading for 15 or 20 minutes then:
- make a few summary notes;
- have a quick stretch or get a drink;
- go on to the next section.

Did this help your concentration and understanding? You may need to try reading for 10 minutes before taking a short break. Experiment with different chunks of time. The time of day and what you are reading will probably affect your reading time span.

You can always use any odd minutes you find you have spare. Use short chunks of free time to prepare for a larger reading task:

- get all the reading material together in one place;
- make sure you have other things you need: soft pencil, highlighter, notepaper, recorder, ruler, dictionary;
- go through the piece and decide the sections you need to read.

Now you are well prepared to start the task when you have more time.

Reading aloud

In our opinion, no one should ever be put in the position of having to read aloud but sometimes it is unavoidable. Fears often stem from school, where children may have had to read aloud in front of others.

- *I hated being asked to read out loud at school as I was so anxious about pronouncing the words correctly.*
- *I used to play truant on days where we had to read out loud to the class.*
- *I used to try and memorize the whole passage so I could appear to be reading my bit.*

Although it is generally thought that this is only a major problem for young dyslexics at school, comments from dyslexic adults suggest that the problem persists into adulthood.

- *I worried about tutorials in case I had to read a bit out.*
- *I hate meetings, in case I have to read something aloud.*

Reading aloud to other adults

Employing strategies for reading aloud are more limited unless you tell people that you are dyslexic or have a reading difficulty. There are many reasons why people do not like reading aloud and therefore it is acceptable to politely refuse. However, if you're prepared to have a go you can:

- at least prepare your bit and practise;
- read and record so that you can listen to it;
- even try to memorize it – for ideas on memorizing see Chapter 10.

Before a meeting, offer to do a particular part so you are in control of your contribution.

Reading to children

Don't feel you can't do this – there's magic in turning over pages together.

- Practise first on their favourite books – you could then record them.
- Listen to the recordings together.
- Use talking books and listen together.

This can be fun and you'll be reading at an easier level, which will help you to improve your fluency. Poetry can be easier: poems such as those by Dr Seuss are rhythmic, repetitive, good for your phonological awareness (see Chapter 1) and children love them!

Sir Steve Redgrave (Olympic oarsman and also dyslexic) said:

> Now that I have children, I want to make sure that they can read and write well. I spend a lot of time reading to them and, as a result, my own reading has improved too.

If you still feel a bit nervous about reading to children, do what people did before books – use your imagination and make up stories.

Using a library

Libraries can be complicated places. Most people, dyslexic or not, have to ask for help at some time. Our advice is to treat the library much as you would a department store or supermarket – if you can't find what you want, ask for help. Most libraries have electronic indexes on a computer. For example, if you're looking for an article in a journal, take a quick look at the index and then ask if you can't find it. If you are going to use the library a lot, ask for guidance on how to use the index. Ask them for a printed copy of the instructions so that you can refer to them again. You can access libraries online these days so you can do some of the searching before you get there.

Fiction books will be in alphabetical order by the author's surname so take your alphabet arc with you (printable document **1** on our online resource). Non-fiction will be divided up into subsections such as travel, science, hobbies, etc. These will be further divided; for example, travel will be divided into continents and then subdivided into countries. The reference section can be very useful for encyclopaedias, directories, newspapers, journals, brochures, CD-ROMs etc.

Borrowing books from public libraries is free and internet access is usually available. If they don't have the book you are interested in, you can ask them to get it for you from another library. Libraries give you the opportunity to read books you don't want to buy, read books you might want to buy and read books that are no longer available to buy. Students may find university libraries particularly helpful. Many libraries have extra facilities for dyslexic readers such as longer loan periods, so ask for information.

In this chapter

In this chapter we have looked at:
- why we need to read;
- the processes involved in reading summarized from Chapter 1;
- the kind of problems that can make reading difficult;
- strategies to help you with reading and comprehension;
- reading aloud and using a library.

We hope that you can now:
- understand a bit more about how you read and what you need to read;
- see how you can be more selective in what you read;
- find ways of improving your comprehension;
- get more enjoyment from your reading.

6

Getting down what you want to say

Writing is easy. All you do is stare at a blank sheet of paper until drops of blood form on your head.
(Gene Fowler, journalist)

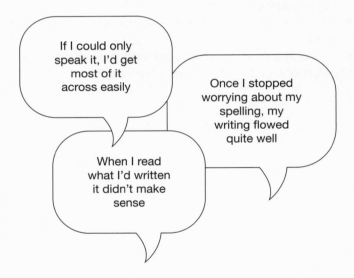

If I could only speak it, I'd get most of it across easily

Once I stopped worrying about my spelling, my writing flowed quite well

When I read what I'd written it didn't make sense

In this chapter we look at:
- the tasks involved in writing;
- how you can break it down into smaller, more manageable chunks;
- strategies that can help you, many that have been devised by dyslexic people;
- what help is available.

Figure 6.1 The two sides of writing

Where do you start?

You have something you need to write. You also have lots of ideas and a blank sheet of paper. Where do you start? Why might writing be difficult for you? Writing is a complex task – in fact, it is a complex collection of tasks that can be split into two groups – see Figure 6.1. These tasks need to be broken down to get started.

The writing task

What is different about spoken and written language?

Spoken language is different from written language. Some of these differences are very subtle. Look at the example of a written transcript of spontaneous speech.

Here is comedian Jimmy Tarbuck talking about the Beatle George Harrison:

> *He used to play his guitar . . . and he'd have a cigarette on one of the strings . . . er . . . you know . . . when they tie the string to top of the guitar and the strings would be loose . . . he'd sometimes have a cigarette . . . and he was . . . um . . . a heavy smoker when he was younger.*

In speech we shorten phrases like 'he would' to 'he'd' and we put in expressions like 'you know'. We may also wave our hands about, use different voice tones, put emphasis on words and make facial expressions to help convey the meaning. These options are not available when we write things down so we need to use other ways of conveying meaning such as sentences and punctuation. The words written down are not so very different to the spoken words. The ideas are the same. It is the *conventions* that are different. Writing is more complex.

 ACTIVITY 12
Creative tasks and conventions

Figure 6.2 shows that there are a lot of tasks to cope with! But you don't have to tackle them all at once. Some of these tasks are creative ones and others are about the conventions of writing.

Try sorting them into these two groups using Figure 6.3. We have done a couple for you.

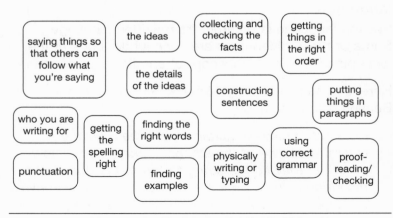

Figure 6.2 Tasks involved in writing

Creative tasks	Conventions
the details of the ideas	*punctuation* *spelling*

Figure 6.3 For use with Activity 12

Breaking down the task

Why is writing complex?

Just consider all the things you have to think about, shown in Figure 6.1.

In Figure 6.4 you can see how we have grouped the tasks. Writing breaks down into two groups of tasks. We've called them Composition and Transcription.

1 Composition is *creative*: the gathering of ideas.
2 Transcription is based on *conventions*, for example correct spelling and punctuation.

It is best to concentrate on the creative tasks first – don't worry about spelling, punctuation, grammar etc. until you have put all your ideas down on paper. If it helps, you can also forget about the act of writing by recording what you want to say!

Creative tasks – composition	Conventions – transcription
• the ideas • the details of the ideas • collecting and checking the facts • finding examples • getting things in the right order	• physical act of writing or typing • constructing sentences • saying things so that others can follow what you are saying • finding the right words • getting the spelling right • putting things in paragraphs • punctuating • using correct grammar • proofreading and checking

Figure 6.4 Answer for Activity 12

What do you want to write?

Everyday life involves lots of writing tasks. The table in Figure 6.5 lists some of the common writing tasks and some strategies to try out. The rest of the chapter looks at other ideas that dyslexic people have found useful. Think of these as tools in your writing toolbox. Try them out and adapt them to suit you. First we'll look at handling your ideas, then we'll look at the conventions. Use this table to help you identify the strategies you could use for a particular task.

Writing task	Strategies to try
Memos, messages and emails	• Bullet points • Templates • Spell checker
Keeping records	Use symbols and colour to represent things
Letters: formal, informal, congratulations, condolences, lobbying, to the local paper, complaints, job applications	• Making simple plans • Capture ideas by recording them • Using samples or templates • Spelling and grammar checkers
Completing forms	Recording yourself reading the questions and your answers, and then listening
Curricula vitae (CVs) and references for people	• Using samples or templates • Planning • Capture ideas by recording them
Minutes of meetings	Using samples or templates
Presentations	• Planning • Capture ideas by recording them
• Articles: for a club magazine or in-house newspaper • Reports: for work, for your interest groups, for a pressure group • Essays, dissertations and theses	• Planning • Capture ideas by recording them • Templates • Spelling and grammar checkers

Figure 6.5 Summary of writing strategies

Your toolbox: some strategies to help with planning

If you are finding your writing task daunting, it's probably because it's a complex piece: a difficult letter, an essay or a report. The task needs breaking down. You can use the ideas in this section for all kinds of writing but they are especially useful for the complicated work.

Figure 6.6 gives you the various stages in the creative side of your writing. Use this to identify the stages that you need to go through and which we will describe. Note-making supports the creative task. You need written notes as a way of keeping your information in one place rather than in lots of books open at different pages. You need notes to summarize your ideas but they do not have to involve lots of writing (see section on *note making* later in this chapter).

☆ Make a plan

Whatever the writing task, making a plan will make it easier. Planning helps to break down the task of doing something you don't like doing or are finding overwhelming. This is the most important stage and is well worth spending the extra time on. Research has shown that the best writers spend more time on the planning stage.

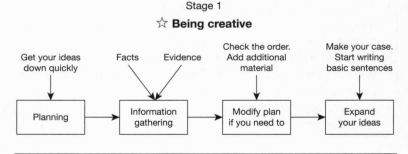

Figure 6.6 The creative tasks

Getting your ideas down

- You can capture your ideas directly onto paper by just jotting them down as they occur to you.
- Try capturing your ideas quickly on a recorder and then transfer them from your recording to your document.
- If you like working on a computer, use planning software (see Chapter 11) to capture your thoughts.

Getting your ideas sorted

The next stage is to get your ideas sorted. Group your ideas together logically and in a sensible order.

- If your ideas have been captured on one large sheet of paper, you can use coloured highlighters to sort them – a different colour for each topic.
- If you used sticky notes, then you can group them together on a large sheet of paper, table or even a wall. Each group should have a common theme or topic.
- If you are using planning software, this will also help you to collect similar ideas together.

If you find a blank sheet of paper scary you could start off by drawing a blank spider or tree diagram or a blank list like the ones in Figure 6.7 – use whatever works best for you. You can then start capturing your ideas.

☆ Information gathering

Note that we have put 'planning' first. You don't have to get the information together before planning! Having a plan helps you to identify the information you need, so use your plan to guide you. If you have used colour coding for each topic on your plan, you can use the same colour scheme to mark the information. The information can be kept in matching coloured folders.

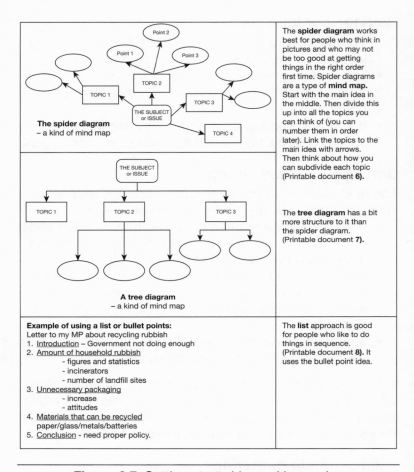

The **spider diagram** works best for people who think in pictures and who may not be too good at getting things in the right order first time. Spider diagrams are a type of **mind map.** Start with the main idea in the middle. Then divide this up into all the topics you can think of (you can number them in order later). Link the topics to the main idea with arrows. Then think about how you can subdivide each topic (Printable document **6).**

The **tree diagram** has a bit more structure to it than the spider diagram. (Printable document **7).**

Example of using a list or bullet points:
Letter to my MP about recycling rubbish
1. Introduction – Government not doing enough
2. Amount of household rubbish
      - figures and statistics
      - incinerators
      - number of landfill sites
3. Unnecessary packaging
      - increase
      - attitudes
4. Materials that can be recycled
    paper/glass/metals/batteries
5. Conclusion - need proper policy.

The **list** approach is good for people who like to do things in sequence. (Printable document **8).** It uses the bullet point idea.

Figure 6.7 Getting started by making a plan
(Examples and blank diagrams can be found in the *Writing* and *Printable documents* sections of our online resource)

☆ Modify your plan and add detail

You may want to alter your plan at this stage for various reasons:

- You have found some new and relevant information.
- You find you need to divide one of your topics into two or more topics.

- Check back to your original task – are you still on the right track?
- Check that your topics are in the right order.

Make the changes you need.

☆ Expanding and explaining your ideas

Now you have your plan and some notes, you can begin to expand on your ideas to include more detail if you feel it necessary.

- Take each topic separately. Make a list of relevant points, using phrases or short sentences.
- Expanding simple sentences: try writing short sentences to begin with, each covering one point. You may find it easier to write these as a list first to make sure that you include all the details. If you find this difficult, record it first.
- Don't forget that you will also need to think about your introduction and conclusion – even a letter might need to have these, though they will probably be very short.

Backing up what you are saying

Generally, in writing you will need to make a case for something:

- in a letter of complaint;
- in a job application – as evidence of your capabilities;
- in a memo – to ensure that people act on your request;
- in record keeping – so that you or others will know why a decision was made;
- in a reference you write about someone;
- in an essay.

Making your point is probably the most important thing to think about. After all, why should people believe you without any evidence? How can they understand the point?

Your case should:	Strategies to use:
• be consistent	Check there are no contradictions in what you say
• explain any evidence that you are using	Say where you found the evidence
• distinguish between fact and opinion	Ask yourself: can it be proved or is it just an opinion?

Figure 6.8 Making a good case

Making sure that you have made a good case needs a few simple strategies. We give some ideas in the table below. There are more detailed ideas for *Making a case* in the *Writing* section of our online resource. Make sure you have all the facts for backing up your case.

By now we hope you can see that the writing task can be broken down into creative tasks and transcription tasks. Concentrate on getting and organizing the ideas first.

Your toolbox: some strategies to help with writing

The conventions of writing broadly cover all those transcription tasks – the different stages involved in getting our ideas down on paper in a way that they can be understood clearly by others. Thinking about these tasks can get in the way of ideas, so don't concentrate on grammar, spelling, punctuation etc., until you are happy that you have collected most of your ideas together.

In Figure 6.9 we suggest how to get going on transcription. There are more ideas in the *Writing* section of our online resources.

Stage 2
★ **Dealing with the conventions**

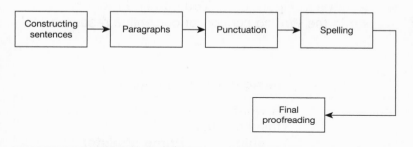

Figure 6.9 The transcription tasks: the conventions

★ Strategies for constructing sentences

If you have all the points you want to make in your planning diagram you can now begin to write. Recording can be very useful as it allows you to rehearse what you want to say and copy down the best version. When you speak, sentences come relatively easily. When you write, you may have to remember that sentences should have a subject and a verb . . .

Subject – A noun or a pronoun	Verb
The Prime Minister They The ship	spoke were running will sail

Figure 6.10

. . . but will usually include a lot more:

The new Prime Minister spoke for over half an hour about the economy.

If you think you have difficulty writing grammatically correct sentences, make them simple first. Then you can add in more detail by using different parts of speech that we describe in Figure 6.11. You can find more *parts of speech* in the *Writing* section of our online resource.

Basic parts of speech	
noun	A word that is the name of a person, thing or quality: **ship** **Prime Minister** **John** **computer** **idea**
pronoun	A word used in place of a noun usually to avoid repeating the noun: **it** **they** **you** **him** *The ship will sail. It leaves on Monday.*
verb	A word that expresses an action or a state. It is a 'doing' or 'being' word: **spoke** **were running** **stands**
adjective	A word used to describe a noun or pronoun: **old** **pretty** **blue** **large** *The large ship will sail.*
adverb	A word used with a verb to add to or modify the meaning: **quickly** **softly** **pleasantly** *They were running quickly.*

Figure 6.11 Examples of parts of speech

★ Strategies for paragraphs

Paragraphs need:

- one central theme or idea;
- to start with a pointer sentence that answers the question: what is this paragraph all about?

Everything in the paragraph must relate to its central theme. Finish with a concluding sentence that either summarizes or sums up the paragraph or leads to the next one. Figure 6.12 is a visual representation of what a paragraph should contain:

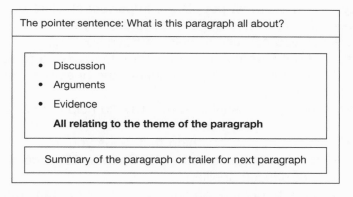

Figure 6.12 Visual representation of a paragraph

There are two important paragraphs to remember: the introduction and conclusion. Almost every piece of writing needs these – many people find it easier to write the introduction last *but* you do need to make sure you are still on track – check the original purpose.

The introduction should tell your reader what you are *intending to say*. The conclusion should briefly summarize *what you have said* and link to your introduction. It may start with 'In summary . . .' or include 'From the information described, the conclusion is . . .' It might also say something about what you think is the next step, such as future action to be taken by someone else.

★ Strategies for spelling

Spelling only became rule-bound in the 18th century. Before then, people were much less concerned with spelling consistently.

Spelling is one of the biggest concerns for dyslexic people mainly because people are often judged by the way they spell. Most people are imperfect spellers or make mistakes when under pressure. Here are some strategies you can use to help improve spelling:

- Find out some of the more common spelling rules. Find creative ways to remember the ones that you find useful.
- Make words visual in some way, to help imprint a spelling on your mind.
- A rhyme, a pun, anything that helps you to remember (mnemonics – see Chapter 10) to remind you of difficult spellings.
- Make a bookmark on stiff paper or card, and write key words on it. This is useful for jargon or technical words.
- Your personal dictionary – collect words you want to remember in a notebook or on index cards. Keep it in your pocket and refer to it when you have a spare minute.
- Use a spellchecker – hand-held or on a computer (see Chapter 11).
- Write words you frequently misspell on large pieces of paper with brightly coloured pens and stick them up around the house – see the cartoon.
- Try using a spelling dictionary such as the Ace Spelling Dictionary (see Appendix B), which groups words by how they sound.

For more about these strategies with examples, including the Multi-sensory Spelling Programme for Priority Words (MUSP), see the *Spelling* section of our online resource.

If you have difficulty looking words up in dictionaries and other reference books that are arranged in alphabetical order, try an alphabet arc, Figure 6.13. It can be kept folded up in your pocket for quick reference. This is one of the most popular strategies used by dyslexic people. You can print a copy from our online resource, printable document **1**.

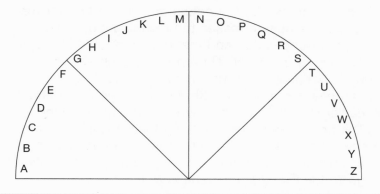

Figure 6.13 Alphabet arc

✍ ACTIVITY 13
Why is punctuation important?

Read the following passage to see why punctuation is important:

> *bill and jane are going to paris on tuesday for a long weekend it will be their first visit so they have bought several guidebooks to give them an idea of what to see jane says bill wont want to spend too much time in art galleries but they both agree that the louvre is essential*

Punctuation:

- Makes things easier to read.

For example, even if we are not good at punctuation, we expect to see capital letters in the right places: Bill and Jane are going to Paris on Tuesday.

- Makes the meaning clear.

Who won't want to spend too much time in art galleries?

- *Jane says, Bill won't want to spend too much time in art galleries.*
- *Jane, says Bill, won't want to spend too much time in art galleries.*

So we can see that punctuation is important for the reader because it makes the meaning clear. We expect punctuation and feel uncomfortable if it is missing or incorrect. Thinking too much about punctuation as you write is likely to get in the way of ideas and interfere with the flow – you may find it easier to write first and then add the punctuation. The first three punctuation marks in Figure 6.14 are the most important so here is some advice about using them. For further advice and more information go to the *Punctuation* section of our online resource.

★ Strategies for punctuation

. Full stop ('stop' or' period')

Full stops mark the end of a sentence. Use them more than you expect to – if you are in any doubt use a full stop. This helps to avoid long rambling sentences.

Full stops should be used with abbreviations: for example, *p.t.o.* They are often dropped in common abbreviations, particularly those with capital letters (called acronyms): *BBC, MP, AA, EU.*

? Question mark

Use a question mark every time there is a genuine direct question:

> *Are you going?*

but not in reported questions:

> *I asked if he was going.*

, Commas

A comma gives a slight pause in a sentence. Like twins, they often come in pairs so that they can separate out ideas in a sentence. But don't include too many in your sentence – if in doubt, use a full stop. Use commas:

- to separate out something that isn't essential to the sentence:

    > *Hamlet, a tragedy by Shakespeare, is a long play.*

- to separate items in a list:

    > *My journey will take me through France, Belgium, the Netherlands and Germany.*

.	full stop ('stop' or 'period')
?	question mark
,	comma
!	exclamation mark
'	apostrophe
( )	brackets
" "	quotation marks
-	dash
:	colon
;	semicolon

Figure 6.14 Punctuation marks

- to separate out the conditional part of the sentence:

  If you do that, you will miss the bus.

  After we've been to the shops, we can have a cup of coffee.

- to separate out a word that links to the previous sentence:

  However, next year is a leap year.

  Next year is a leap year, however.

ABC Capital letters

You must use capital letters at the start of each sentence and also:

- for a person's name:

  Vicki
  Mrs Robinson
  Dr Thomson

- for trade names and businesses:

  Marks & Spencer

- for names of places:

  East Wittering
  Paris
  Germany

- for streets and rivers:

  10 Downing Street
  River Wye

- for days and months:

  Friday 19th May

- for titles of specific people, organizations, events, courses:

  the Prime Minister
  Friends of the Earth
  the General Election
  Pure Mathematics

- for abbreviations:

  BBC, USA

The best time to check the punctuation is after you
have finished most of the writing

★ Strategies for proofreading – checking what you have written

Proofreading and correcting your errors should be done
last. When you're satisfied with the content and
structure, read through your draft at least twice – once
to check spelling and once for punctuation.

It can be very difficult to spot your own errors, especially if dyslexia affects your visual perception. So here are some strategies to try:

- Concentrate on something different each time you read through: spelling, paragraphing, punctuation.
- You could try reading your work backwards to spot spelling mistakes.
- If you are proofreading on your computer screen, try using the 'zoom' facility at 150 per cent as errors seem to stand out better.
- When proofreading, correct errors immediately when you spot them. Note in the margin or highlight any words you are unsure of – then ask someone or use a dictionary to correct them.
- Read your work from the beginning and look for errors related to your particular difficulties, for example: omitted words, wrong punctuation, or incorrect grammar.
- Try reading your work onto a recorder and playing it back, or use read-back technology. You're likely to hear anything that doesn't make sense.
- Get someone else to proofread as well.

Breaking down the proofreading task

Spread the proofreading over more than one day – several, if possible. Mistakes that you miss on one day often seem to stand out on another. You can print a comprehensive **proofreading checklist** from our online resource, printable document **9**.

★ Strategies for handwriting

The task we need to think about while we transcribe our ideas is handwriting. Many people use word processors these days and this is generally good news for dyslexic people – it makes what you write legible for others as well as for you. But you may not have a computer to hand. Your handwriting may be good but it may take you a long time. Many dyslexic people do not join up letters. They print because they know that everyone will be able to read it. They may have never really mastered joined-up writing.

If your handwriting needs improving, if your hand tires when you write for any length of time or if you try to avoid handwriting, here are a few ideas to help:

- Try different kinds of pen (ball-point, fibre-tip etc.) and colours. Try fatter or thinner pens. Try changing to a different pen while you are writing – a different-shaped pen will use different muscles and help to relieve the strain. Try a pen that flows more easily like some fibre-tips or a fountain pen. Experiment to find the sort that suits you best.
- If you find it hard to keep the size and shape of the letters regular, look for a basic book on handwriting. You can find some strategies in the section about *Handwriting* on our online resource.
- Use squared paper to help keep your writing even.
- Pull the pen over the paper, rather than push it. There's less resistance that way.

A word processor will, of course, spare you the difficulties of handwriting, as well as helping you to avoid spelling errors. Learning to touch-type can be very useful as many words become automatic by locating the letters to the position of the fingers.

A summary of the ideas to help with writing

You should now appreciate that it isn't necessary to think about the conventions of writing until you have collected and ordered all your ideas. You now have a 'toolbox' of strategies and suggestions to deal with ...

- constructing sentences
- constructing paragraphs
- punctuation

- spelling
- checking or proofreading
- handwriting

. . . that have worked for many people. You can adapt these to suit you and the task you have in hand. We want to encourage you to create your own strategies – don't feel that you have to do things the way you were taught if these haven't worked in the past. Try something new.

Perhaps you'll get to grips with all the conventions and get all the transcription right but remember – it means nothing without the good ideas.

Colourless green ideas sleep furiously.

Written work can be perfect, grammatically clear and concise – and totally without meaning – as Professor Noam Chomsky demonstrates in the sentence above!

Note making: a particular kind of writing skill

This is a good moment to look at how to make notes. Notes should be a summary. They can be visual and diagrammatic. You can use colour and abbreviations. See Figure 6.15 for some ideas. For more on how to make mind maps, you can refer to the *Writing* section of our online resource.

You may need to make notes:
- in meetings;
- at talks or lectures;
- from radio or TV;
- from books.

In the first three situations you will have very little time to make notes, let alone practise some strategies. If you are given a handout, add notes to this. It is always worth asking for one. You have more time if you are making notes from books – so start practising making notes as

1. **Mind maps** – on a separate sheet of paper, pick out the key points as words, phrases or short sentences.	
2. **Marking text,** either by underlining or highlighting: use a highlighter pen to mark key words and phrases.	You have to be very selective – otherwise you'll highlight everything! Decide what's really important
3. **Summing up** each paragraph in one sentence.	This takes practice – but combine it with the next idea…
4. **Making a recording.**	Say in your own words what you think you have understood from what you have just read. Imagine that you are telling someone about it – but you haven't got much time so you have to give them the gist.
5. **Question** as you go – your notes can be the answers to your questions.	How? What? Why? Where? Who?

Figure 6.15 Ideas for note making

you read, using one or more of the suggested strategies. This will help you to improve your concentration and comprehension while learning how to make notes at the same time. Try using a spider diagram, adding a new 'leg' for each new topic. Try developing your own abbreviations as a kind of shorthand. Try using visual reminders such as stars, arrows, simple drawings. Only write down one or two word memory joggers.

Possible sources of help with writing

Help from people

Here are some ideas as to how other people can help, including close friends, family, tutors and colleagues. You don't have to tell anyone that you are dyslexic if

you don't want to; many people struggle with writing. You can just ask them to do specific things using phrases such as:
- Does this make sense to you?
- Would you mind double checking this for me?

- To help with getting your ideas down, ask someone to write down the gist of what you are saying. There is no need to dictate as that is a skill in itself. Find someone who can write quickly and can capture the feel of what you are saying.
- Ask someone to check your work. If you know the person well you can ask them not to do the corrections but just to indicate any errors for you to find and correct – this is a good learning exercise.
- If you are a student you could ask your tutor to mark up part or all of your work indicating errors rather than correcting them.

Computers
Word-processing packages on computers help you cope with many tasks you might find difficult or time-consuming. Technology isn't everything but Chapter 11 gives you an idea of what is available. A computer can be a real boon for writing tasks. Consider the following benefits:
- It compensates for your overloaded working memory because you can get things down quickly.
- You can move things around easily – there is no need for endless rewriting.
- Your writing is legible, neat and you don't have to think about letter formation.
- Inbuilt spellcheckers correct most spelling errors and many grammatical errors too.
- Read-back software can help with proofreading and voice-activated software can type in the words as you speak.

These are only some of the benefits but don't just take our word for it. There are a number of places where you can try out equipment without pressure – see Chapter 11.

Pause for a moment

Look at these two statements. Which would you prefer to hear?

Here is a terrible piece of work – look at the spelling and punctuation!

Or

This is quite an interesting piece of work – quite a few typos though!

Both statements were made by the same person about the same piece of work. The first piece of work was handwritten; the second was typed but had exactly the same errors (typos = typing mistakes).

Other sources of help

There are many sources of published sample letters, reports, CVs, references. You can find such samples or templates in many books or on various websites. A template gives you an outline for you to fill in your own details. Ask in a good bookshop or search on the internet.

Some professional writers or scribes will, for a fee, write down from your dictation. Ghost writers will write the text in their own words from what you tell them.

We hope that by reading this chapter you now feel that there are many ways of getting down your ideas. Take a deep breath and have a go. Don't sit and stare at a blank piece of paper. The author, Mary Vorse, once said 'The art of writing is the art of applying the seat of the pants to the seat of the chair!'

In this chapter

In this chapter we have discussed how to:

- gain a better understanding of what writing involves;
- break down the task into smaller, more manageable tasks;
- try some new strategies to help with writing;
- be aware of the help that is available;
- see that writing can be rewarding.

Some of these suggestions should save you a bit of time and make writing a little easier. Adapt them to suit you and the way you think and work!

7

Getting done what you want to do

Being organized helps you wrestle back the controls from life.

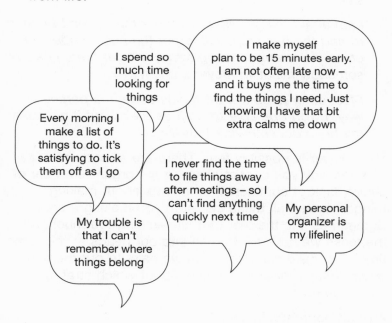

I spend so much time looking for things

I make myself plan to be 15 minutes early. I am not often late now – and it buys me the time to find the things I need. Just knowing I have that bit extra calms me down

Every morning I make a list of things to do. It's satisfying to tick them off as I go

I never find the time to file things away after meetings – so I can't find anything quickly next time

My trouble is that I can't remember where things belong

My personal organizer is my lifeline!

In this chapter we look at ideas for organizing time and the things you may have to get done. You will see that a lot of the strategies are similar to many of the ideas discussed in previous chapters. You should be getting the feeling that strategies fall into groups with common themes: multi-sensory, chunking, making things memorable, etc. This should help you when you are trying to think of ways to do things or how to begin a task.

How you do things now

Pause for a moment

Why don't things go right? Look at these quotes from dyslexic people. What is the feeling common to them all?

> *I'm so scared that I will get things in the wrong order and not do my bit at the right time that I feel almost sick.*

> *I am afraid things will go wrong – that I won't be able to find the bus stop, will forget the bus number, will go to the wrong meeting room, will get there late, will somehow fail at whatever it is anyway.*

> *I feel other people want things done in a particular way. I won't be able to do it as they want it because my brain doesn't work that way.*

The answer is possibly fear. There are all sorts of reasons why you cannot seem to get organized. Fear of failure, lack of confidence, concerns about making things worse – all these can stop you making a start. Sometimes it is the fear of it all seeming too much. All the tasks we have to do rush into our heads at the same time – to make sense of them we have to put them in order. Take a moment to think about which strategies would be useful here.

A good approach involves:
- Chunking – breaking down the task into smaller tasks.
- Planning – getting the smaller tasks into the right order.

This gets you started and ensures some success.

ACTIVITY 14
Finding out what works for you

In this activity we want to help you identify some of the organization skills you use successfully and some of the things you leave to chance.

Think of an occasion when you had to meet a deadline. For example:

- getting to a new destination on time;
- making a wedding cake;
- filling in your tax form;
- organizing a training session or workshop.

Jot down your answers to the following questions:

- What planning did you do to ensure that you met the deadline?
- What resources and information did you use?
- Who else was involved?
- How did you make sure that they did their part?
- Did you meet the deadline?
- If not, what went wrong?
- What could you do next time to make things work better?

You can print a blank form for this activity – printable document **4** on our online resource. You may find it useful to do this activity more than once, for example, for something that worked well and for something that was a bit of a disaster. Then you can compare your answers for both.

Take some time to answer the last of these questions. You'll need to look at your answers to the others first. You may not be able to come up with the right ideas straight away, but read on and then come back to the question to see if some of the things we suggest can be adapted to suit you.

Two examples of difficulties with organization

Example 1: Dealing with new equipment

Most people don't read instructions or those lengthy computer manuals mainly because many are badly written. Instead they work it out as they go.

Here is one person's account of the struggle to cope with written instructions:

I'm afraid to read instructions in case I can't follow them. Unless they are printed in fairly large letters and they don't look too long or complicated, I'm likely to give up.

So I 'dash' at the task, pressing every button in the vain hope it will do what I want. And yes, it is true that if I slow down and calmly talk myself into looking it up and writing down in a list what I have to do first – then I can help myself.

It has taken me so many painful experiences to realize that organization is worthwhile. I am enthusiastic and impatient – sometimes with wonderful intuition! But I can't rely on that every time.

Here are some ideas that could help:
- Set time aside to spend on that manual and highlight the bits that look useful to you.
- If the information is available electronically (and many manuals are these days), change the font and the background colour to suit you.
- Try writing your own instructions as you go – in your own words rather than in technical jargon. But, put those manuals in a safe place so that you can find them if you need them.
- 'If you don't use it, you lose it.' Things that you do regularly are easier to remember.

Example 2: Preparation for an interview

And here is another person who has made some attempt to get organized, despite real fears:

> *I've got an interview in Birmingham. I'm worried about finding the place, getting there in good time and not forgetting any of the paperwork – and I've got to prepare for the interview. It all seems overwhelming.*

> *I've got the times of the trains but I don't know how far the place is from the station. I'm worried I won't have enough time to get there – I could take a taxi. I've got to take some examples of my work with me but I can't decide what. What shall I wear? I must get my jacket cleaned – will there be time?*

 ACTIVITY 15
How long does it take?

Do you know exactly how long it takes you to do particular tasks? Time a few tasks and keep a note using the chart in Figure 7.1. Try some of these. Estimate the time – then time yourself and see if you are right.

Many dyslexic people do not have a strong sense of time passing. How close was your estimate to the actual time? If it is less than the actual time, you need to be more realistic as to how much time you need to allow for many tasks.

This is how you might get started for something similar:
- Make a list of everything you need to take with you, including tickets, umbrella, money etc. To make your list, use visualization: imagine the whole

journey in steps, noting at each stage what you will need.

- Check the train times, get tickets in advance.
- Set aside some time to look at the road or street map of the area. Get or print a copy and highlight your route from the station and work out how long it might take.
- To prepare for the interview: choose examples of your work that give a good cross-section of your skills.

Task	Estimate	Actual time taken
To clean the car		
To walk to your station or bus stop		
To do the weekly shop		
To mow the lawn		
Add some of your own: _____ _____ _____ _____ _____ _____		

Figure 7.1 For use with Activity 15

> Take time to plan and prepare.
> Break the task down into smaller tasks.
> Get things in the right order.

Organizing time

Many tasks take dyslexic people longer to complete, particularly those involving reading and writing.

Strategies to organize your time

- Make an overall plan – see Chapter 6 for mind maps etc.
    - Include the aims and dates for deadlines.
    - Identify all the tasks.
    - Identify in which order things have to be done.
- Make a wall chart showing several weeks: put the 'week beginning' dates along the top and the tasks to be done down the side.
    - Mark on the chart the deadlines.
    - Don't forget to fix a finish date for tasks that have to be done before another task can start.
    - And don't forget to allow enough time!
- Each week, make a 7-day chart.
    - Put the days along the top and hours or morning/afternoon/evening down the side.
    - You can print a blank chart from our online resource, printable document **11**).
    - Put it in a prominent place.
    - Write in all your other commitments first.
    - Slot the other things you want to do into the time that's free.

Figure 7.2 expresses these ideas in a visual way.

Try it for a week and see how it goes. See how it helps you.

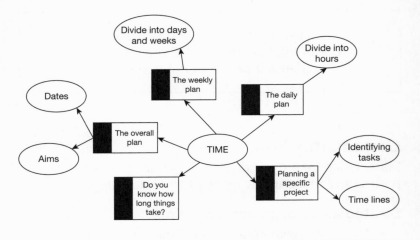

Figure 7.2 Strategies using time to plan for important things

Organizing things

Some strategies to organize your things

Paperwork is likely to be the most difficult thing to organize – it involves words and reading. Again planning is the key. And, if you keep your plan, you can use it for reference – 'where did I put that dry cleaner's receipt?'

Figure 7.3 is a plan we did for household information – set out as a mind map – and Figure 7.4 shows the same plan as a list. You may like to add to or adapt them for your own use.

Summary of useful strategies

Breaking down what you need to do into steps helps with organization. Here are some ideas that have worked for others – some may be useful for you. Adapt them as you want. Highlight the useful ones and add a few of your own.

- For planning: mind maps (see Chapter 6 and the *Writing* section of the online resource), lists, wall charts – you can buy excellent ones that come with sticky stars and spots in different colours, or you can design your own.
- For planning and remembering: Filofax™, diary (the biggest you can carry around), electronic organizers, lists.
- For storing and organizing paper: files of all kinds and in different colours: box files, lever arch files, ring binders, folders and wallets, plastic wallets. Keep a supply of sticky labels for renaming used files.
- Put colour to good use – keep to the same colour for the same things, e.g. for all your financial things use yellow labels on files, use yellow files and document cases, yellow highlighters, yellow plastic pegs to keep things together and so on.
- For time: set your watch, mobile phone, electronic organizer, timer, alarm clock, time management software, timeline charts (e.g. *Gantt charts* described in our online resource), relations, friends and colleagues, and allow extra time.
- For storing and organizing information: card index, filing systems, the folder system on your computer, make a recording.
- For prioritizing: filing trays, review of previous lists.
- For coping with procedures: write instructions in your own words as you do things; flow diagrams etc.
- For organizing objects and things: create a specific place. Look for unused spaces and attractive storage boxes.

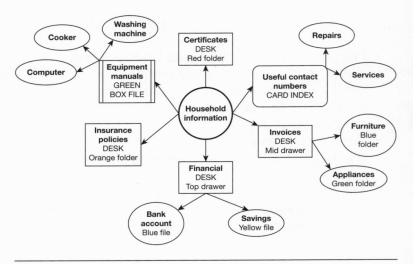

Figure 7.3 Example of a mind map for organizing a household filing system

GREEN BOX FILE:
Equipment manuals
    Computer
    Cooker
    Washing machine

CARD INDEX:
Useful contact numbers
    Repairs
    Services

DESK:
    Red folder: Certificates
    Orange folder: Insurance policies
Middle drawer: Invoices
    Blue folder: Furniture
    Green folder: Appliances
Top drawer: Financial
    Yellow file: Savings
    Blue file: Bank account

Figure 7.4 List for organizing household filing system

An example:

> *My diary is a life line. I divide each page into 2 columns; one is for work lists, meetings etc., and the other one for home time – yoga class, note for me to pick up someone at 7.00 etc. Every day I use the diary for work and I am then reminded of the other things to do later. I can also plan ahead, so when I think of something I can jot it into a day some weeks ahead.*

 ACTIVITY 16
What do you need to organize?

This activity is a bit like making a New Year's resolution. We want you to identify something in your life that needs organizing and then plan how to go about it.

First, ask yourself what you want to organize.

Take a look at Figure 7.5, which gives two examples. Print out a blank table from the online resource, printable document **3**. Add something you want to organize.

Think of some strategies that might work. You can use or adapt any of those we've suggested in this chapter but hopefully you may come up with something creative of your own.

What I want to organize	Strategies
I want to take all the right things with me to work each day.	• Stick **a list** to the front door. Put the standard items at the top and leave room for things you need occasionally. • **Collect everything** together by the door the night before.
I want to get fit to run a marathon.	• **Make a plan:** type of exercise/type of diet. • **Gather information:** costs of facilities, clothing, hours of opening of gym. • **Make a chart:** Identify the time required. Find space in your life. • **Set up reminders:** timer on your watch or mobile phone. Sticky notes. • **Make a chart:** to measure your progress.

Figure 7.5 For use with Activity 16

Other things to think about

Priorities

While it is important to stick to your list or plan, if something goes wrong you may need to change your priorities and even leave some things out. If you find you have less time than you planned for, you have to let some things go. This kind of flexibility can be hard for some dyslexic people. It's essential then to have a Plan A (the original) and a Plan B to cope with the unexpected. Plan B should consist of the most important things in Plan A.

Because things can take you much longer, make sure you:
- allow enough time;
- have a good plan and a 'Plan B';
- understand what is expected of you;
- don't waste time on non-essential things;
- don't go off at a tangent – stay focused;
- don't panic!

In this chapter

In this chapter we have encouraged you to think about:
- how you organize time and things you have to do;
- what it is you want to organize;
- some useful ideas to adapt to suit you.

8

Self-esteem and motivation

In this chapter we consider why self-esteem is important. We give suggestions for things that people with dyslexia can do to improve self-esteem and gain confidence in approaching tasks and opportunities.

Introduction

> *Virtually all the essential aspects of self-esteem are tied to the ways in which the world has related to us in the past and is currently related to us.*
>
> (Social psychologist, W.B. Swann)

Over time we develop our self image – who we think we are. We build it up from how we feel, how we look, how we do various things and what skills we have. We get an overall sense of our competence at various skills and of what other people think of us as a friend, a student, a parent, a colleague etc. We make judgements on our value: 'I'm good at music but I'm not very good at sport.' We get feelings about our value from:

- our own sense of our competence; and
- from that given to us by others.

Our self-esteem is made up of all these feelings about ourselves. Sometimes we may say: 'I feel quite good about myself generally – I am really quite good at some things.' The fact we are not so good at something else doesn't really damage our self–esteem overall: 'I don't feel badly about not being able to sky-dive but reading aloud is another matter.'

As children we are especially influenced by our parents and by our experiences at school. We may take the opinions of teachers very seriously and take them on as our own opinions of ourselves. We compare ourselves with other children in the classroom. As adults, if our self-esteem is not very high, we may mistakenly blame ourselves for something that goes wrong. We may keep going on a course of study because someone else has told us to. When we do feel good, however, anything seems possible. So self-esteem is important – it frees up our confidence to have a go. We can learn from mistakes instead of seeing them as being stupid.

Dyslexia and self-esteem

Dyslexic difficulties can affect self-esteem because acquiring literacy skills, in particular, is seen by so many people as being very important. So many areas of interest, both practical and imaginative, are opened up through the written word. If reading is difficult it makes finding out about things a chore and school work a struggle.

Moreover, dyslexic difficulties are not confined to a baffling struggle with reading and writing. They can also affect organization, comprehension, tasks involving time-keeping and memory. You may see these difficulties as annoying inconsistencies but the problem is that others are neither trained to understand nor resourced to deal with such difficulties.

Some common negative attitudes

'I must be careless'

Learners may do better at some tasks on one day compared with another. Inconsistency in performance between different days, times and tasks can mean that you often make mistakes that irritate (busy) people. The more worried you become, the more mistakes

ACTIVITY 17
How good is your self-esteem?

1 What did you enjoy? Circle any that seem true to you and add some of your own:

When I was young I enjoyed:

- cooking
- swimming
- tennis
- dancing
- reading
- listening to stories
- watching television

- playing ball games
- cycling
- football
- playing a musical instrument
- _____
- _____

2 What about now? Circle or add as many of the following as you feel apply to you:

The things I enjoy now are:

- cooking
- driving
- reading
- speaking in small groups
- _____

- singing
- DIY
- travelling
- art
- _____
- _____

3 What do you think others think about you?

I think other people see me as being good at:

- _____
- _____

The things you have circled or added are likely to be the things that you are good at. If you want to find out more about your own perceptions of your abilities and approaches to learning, the book by Robert Burden: *Myself as a Learner* includes a lot on self-esteem, and is readable but expensive. Your local library may have a copy.

follow. Being constantly corrected is bad for self-esteem and confidence.

'I must be lazy or something'

Many children with dyslexia did not achieve their potential at school despite working extremely hard. Often they were labelled as 'lazy' and came to believe that they really weren't working hard enough.

People are not 'lazy'. They may lack motivation to do something for a variety of reasons. It is worth trying to discover why you lack motivation to do something that you need to do. If you understand why you don't want to do it you can then make better choices. You may decide not to do it at all or, if you decide it has to be done, to find better strategies to help you do it.

'I must be stupid'

It is a myth that poor literacy skills are an indication of low intelligence. Poor literacy skills can be the result of many things such as home environment, disrupted schooling, deafness and dyslexia. Some children may get the impression that others think they are 'stupid'. They may have even been told so, perhaps because their spelling and reading are poor.

Decide what it is you want or need to do.

> *I found it was much easier to be REALLY bad at maths. I was in the top class for most subjects so I felt OK about myself. But maths made me feel baffled, and incompetent, so sliding down to the bottom class let me off both trying and failing. It even seemed to make my failure more interesting because it was spectacular failure.*

This is an example of 'avoidance' – it works well in the way that it stops you getting into stressful and depressing situations. Sometimes that can be a useful, but negative strategy. Negative strategies are often easier but maybe you can think of a more positive way of approaching something you really would like to master.

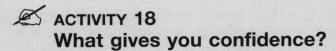

ACTIVITY 18
What gives you confidence?

1 What are the tasks that worry you most now? Make a list below. For some it is reading aloud at a meeting or making a presentation. For others it might be how to handle feelings of panic faced with any challenge.
2 Now what are the tasks that you feel most *confident* doing?
3 What is it about doing these tasks that gives you confidence?

The skills that give you the confidence can be employed with other tasks – they form the basis of strategies that you can use.

Improving confidence and motivation

Some strategies for improving confidence

Build on what you do well

Work to your strengths. Look at your answers to Activity 18. What you have done is identify some of your strengths. Evidence shows that we can be more successful building on the way we do things well rather than correcting faults. Try to think of some more strengths – ask family and friends to help you. You may have a good visual memory or you may be particularly good at dealing with people, for example.

Making mental pictures – visualization

Remember a time or a place where you were doing something or experiencing something in a confident way. Practise recalling that feeling of confidence when you doubt your ability to do something.

Make a model

Look at the thing you want to do and try to imagine the specific steps you need to achieve it. Get someone to explain in detail just how *they* did it. Get them to help you break it down into a series of steps. Many athletes, dancers and musicians rehearse in their heads in addition to physically practising. Recent research shows that mental practice adds enormously to their performance. This is 'visualization'.

Make your thinking positive

It can help to express the thoughts you have about yourself in a different, more positive, way. Some ideas for this are shown in Figure 8.1.

Try constructing another 2 or 3 for yourself now – how can you say something in a different, more positive way?

With practice, expressing your thoughts positively can become automatic. What is more, it's good for you.

Motivation and motivational strategies

You have to feel motivated to do anything – even get up in the morning!

Sometimes when we are motivated we do it for the sake of something or someone. I don't like washing up but if it is to help my friend who broke her arm, I feel motivated and happy to do it. Sometimes we are motivated to do something for better pay or to earn money for a holiday.

When we are deeply motivated we do something for the sake of it, out of enjoyment or interest. We really value whatever it is and that makes it rewarding to do and more fulfilling. This motivation lasts – it might be a particular passion such as painting or a sport.

So – what strategies can you use to develop and maintain motivation?

- Clarify your goals – work out why you want to do it, and remind yourself of the value of doing it.
- Understand why it is important.
- Practice and perseverance have been shown to be more important than basic intellectual ability – believe it! There is now much more evidence that successful people have spent many hours on their particular interest to gain their success.
- Remind yourself of past successes.
- Practise making positive statements – see Figure 8.1.

Your statement:	Your statement expressed more positively:
I am a poor learner.	I sometimes find learning difficult.
I find some aspects of my work impossible to learn.	I can learn these things if they are explained in the right way for me.
This is impossible.	I can tackle this in small chunks.
This will be impossible.	I can do this if I take more time.
I don't think I can do this.	I did this before so I can do it again.

Figure 8.1 Expressing yourself more positively

Tips – for when the motivation dips

- Create a deadline to get you started on a task, as once you get going it can be easier to keep going.
- Decide on one small part of the task and set aside a short period of time where you agree with yourself that you will work on it. This minimizes the sense of 'I can never get it finished in time so it's not worth starting'.
- Reward yourself afterwards.
- Make it fun – be creative. For children, we often get them to make a game of something we want them to do. Try doing the same for yourself.

This is how one person described her experience of dyslexia and her self-confidence:

I was so often ignored when it came to responsible tasks at school and at home that I accepted that I was unreliable and somehow not much good. One day at work I found myself in a long conversation which led to my saying that I supposed perhaps I was quite clever. My colleague expressed amazement that I could have doubted it!

I now realize that I could have done all sorts of things if only I had been shown how; if only I had had the confidence to ask. There were a lot of other things that I was really good at! My confidence is still fragile under stress but I know I have the ability to make the absolute best of all the things I want to do. I just wish I had had the revelation a bit earlier!

Handling change, anxiety and confidence issues

Counsellors can help people make sense of their painful experiences and understand them better. You can ask your GP for details. Counsellors can work with a client on their issues such as low self-esteem and depression that have resulted from not being listened to for a long time.

The strain of being constantly misinterpreted is enormous. Most children develop low self-esteem when they are regularly being criticized because someone is effectively telling them that they are no good (therefore unlovable) whenever they do something the adult doesn't like. Low self-esteem may lead to depression or frustration expressed as anti-social behaviour. Some people may find these frustrations have led to serious problems.

Someone who is dyslexic also has to cope with the fact that they don't necessarily understand why these frustrations are happening to them. They tend to blame themselves when they lose things or turn up late, unaware of the role dyslexia may be playing in this. It will help if a counsellor has some knowledge of dyslexia. If you decide to go and see someone, do tell them. If you are not sure whether you are dyslexic, then explaining the difficulties you have in reading, organizing or remembering will help them work with your feelings about these issues.

It can be enormously helpful to share your feelings about everything that you experience with someone who is independent, and won't judge you. A counsellor's role is to help you to cope more effectively.

In this chapter

In this chapter we have:
- shown why self-esteem is important;
- given suggestions for things that you can do to build up your confidence in everything you do.

9

Handling numbers

Don't skip this chapter if you've always hated numbers, arithmetic and maths. There is something here for you. Everyone needs a little maths – in budgeting, travelling, cooking and DIY. Some of you may need a little maths in your job or some statistics in your course.

In this chapter we start by explaining the root of some of the difficulties. Later we give you a toolbox of strategies to try.

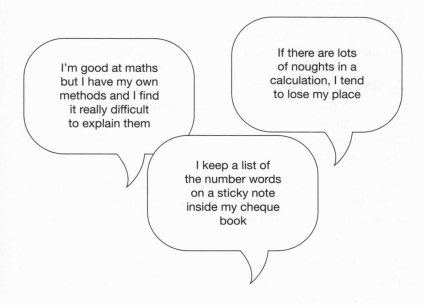

I'm good at maths but I have my own methods and I find it really difficult to explain them

If there are lots of noughts in a calculation, I tend to lose my place

I keep a list of the number words on a sticky note inside my cheque book

Many dyslexics are very good at maths. They have an excellent understanding of the concepts but they may have difficulty with remembering the procedures, the sequence of operations or the times tables. They may have difficulty with the language of maths in the same way as any other aspect of language. You may think you're no good at maths because you've been told so.

Dyscalculia (dis-cal-ku-lee-a)

You will hear the term dyscalculia mentioned. It is a difficulty with the concepts of number and quantity. Some people use the term for dyslexia with numbers. In this case, the difficulties are very similar to the problems that dyslexic people may have with words, but for some people the difficulties only seem to occur with numbers.

In this chapter we address these types of problems. We suggest you refer to the British Dyslexia Association for more details on dyscalculia. On their website select 'about dyslexia', 'schools and colleges', 'dyscalculia'.

Dyslexia and maths

If you are dyslexic you may have taken longer to learn mathematical symbols. These include the numbers themselves, as well as symbols such as + (addition) and x (multiplication).

Much of this can be due to memory: remembering which order to do things in, remembering formulas, remembering the meaning of mathematical words such as 'factorize', 'integrate', 'trigonometry' etc.

Many of the difficulties that you face with words may also arise with numbers (see Figure 9.1) so you can use similar strategies.

Area of difficulty	Effects on literacy (words)	Effects on numeracy (numbers)
Coding and decoding	Relating sounds to letters and letters to sounds Difficulties distinguishing letters such as b and d	Relating numbers, letters and symbols to their meaning Difficulties distinguishing maths notation such as x and +, 6 and 9
Sequencing	Difficulties with the order of the alphabet and months; letters and words in the wrong order	Losing the place when going through a sequence of procedures, getting digits in the wrong order
Memory	Difficulties with spelling	Difficulties with formulas, forgetting instructions. Rote learning difficulties – times tables

Figure 9.1 Comparing some of the effects of dyslexia on words and on numbers

Dyslexic-type problems and strengths

Because many dyslexic people see things holistically and intuitively, they can be very good at making connections and seeing patterns. So those who find ways to overcome the decoding and language difficulties are likely to enjoy and be good at maths.

Coding and decoding

When you look at numbers, letters and symbols, your brain has to decide what they mean. Dyslexia can affect dealing with numbers in two main ways:

- by slowing down the process;
- by causing errors due to forgetting numbers or mistaking one number for another, for example, 6 for 9.

These kinds of difficulty are likely to affect arithmetic but not understanding. Many people who say that they're 'no good at maths', really mean that they have trouble with the arithmetic. And being slower to complete the arithmetic than other people doesn't mean you're less intelligent!

Numbers are codes for quantities: 6 means 6 'things'. Symbols are codes for operations – see Figure 9.2. We know that many dyslexic people have problems with coding and decoding – getting letters and groups of letters wrong. It's the same with numbers and maths symbols.

Procedures: rules and sequencing

The key to learning rules is to understand the processes and how they work.

Most dyslexics also have problems with getting things in the right order. This can cause them to have difficulties with maths, including quite simple arithmetic. Here are some examples:

- Learning multiplication tables.
- Long division involves a sequence of steps. If one step is missed out or in the wrong order, then the answer will be wrong.
- Writing numbers down incorrectly – a dyslexic person may not spot the difference between 1066, 1099, 1660 or 1990; they can look very similar to someone who has sequencing difficulties.
- Problems getting the decimal point in the right place.

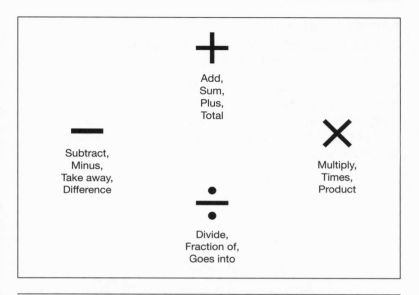

Figure 9.2 Language of mathematical operations (There is a coloured version of this on the online resource)

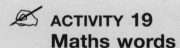 ACTIVITY 19
Maths words

There are other words that mean the same thing as the symbols in Figure 9.2. To which group do you think each of these words belongs?

- decrease
- less than
- division
- more than
- addition

- increase
- share
- power of
- split
- of

- and
- subtraction
- group

Language of maths

Just look at some of the ways we say the same thing in maths, illustrated in Figure 9.2.

So we can see that dealing with the language of numbers can be a source of difficulty. You can find imaginative and creative ways to help you cope. The rest of this chapter gives you some ideas to try. Adapt them or create your own.

Your toolbox: number strategies

Using your learning style

There is more than one way to learn things. Make your learning multi-sensory: draw a diagram *and* listen to the words. Learn by doing something, rather than just reading about it. Relax, make it fun.

Ideas and strategies

Association

Link anything new that you learn to something you already know, for example, linking your bank PIN with a familiar date. Don't forget that you can alter your PIN to a number that is memorable for you – but not anything too obvious like your own birthday! You can reset some combination locks to the number you want.

Calculator

Using a calculator helps to avoid errors with multiplication tables and carrying figures over in sums. But it is possible to make a mistake keying in the numbers, so:

- Do it slowly and twice to see if you get the same answer!
- Say the numbers and operations out loud as you key them in – this will help you to avoid errors.
- Check that your answers are sensible by using the estimation strategy below.

Charts and diagrams

If you have good visual skills, you may find it easier to remember things if you use a chart or diagram. You may be able to use a ready-made one or you could devise your own.

Here is a simple example to illustrate what we mean:

You might want to work out how much carpet to order, or how much paint to buy to decorate a wall. You need the *area*. This means you need to multiply the *length* by the *width* for the carpet, or the *length* by the *height* for the wall. You can use Figure 9.3 to help you remember that to work out the *area* of anything, you take the two dimensions and multiply them.

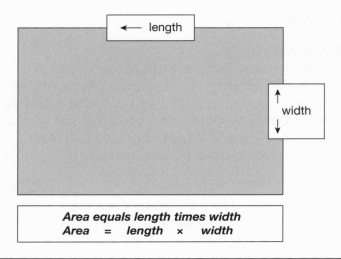

length

width

Area equals length times width
Area = length × width

Figure 9.3 A visual representation of a calculation

This is a basic example, but the idea can be used in quite complicated calculations too.

Chunking

If you need to remember a number, the safest way is to write it down, saying it aloud as you write it, to make sure that you've written it correctly. If you can't write it down, 'chunk' it. Instead of remembering 11 digits for a telephone number, break it down into 5 or 6 numbers. You can link these, if you need to, to personal memorable numbers. Take, for example, the British Dyslexia Association's number 0845 2519002. Remember that:

- all British numbers start with zero (or +44 if you are abroad),
- then memorize:
  eight forty-five, twenty-five, nineteen, zero zero two, *or, for example,*
  the time I leave for work, my age, my house number, zero zero two.

Worked (concrete) examples

Many people find it difficult to remember concepts and theories that are abstract. Having worked examples helps you to understand *and* remember the procedures. For example, you might find it difficult to remember the formula: 'the area of something is the length times the width' – see example in Figure 9.3. But if you think of area as the amount of carpet you need and remember that you have to measure the length and width of the room, this helps to remember the method.

A simple example gives you an idea that you can apply to more complicated situations. A selection of model answers will give you confidence that you are going along the right lines. They can also get you started.

Cuisenaire rods

Cuisenaire rods are small coloured sticks that have a different colour for each length – you may have used them at school. They are excellent for getting the feel of quantity because they can be added together and taken away physically.

Using estimation to check your answer

After you have done your sums, you can ask yourself if you have a sensible answer.

For example:

> Sam had £324.24 in her account. She wrote a cheque for £299.72. She did a written calculation and thought she had £172.52 left! She could have done a rough estimate by saying that the cheque was about £300 and then realized that she only had about £25 left.

Personal dictionary or glossary

New maths words or symbols that you come across could go in your personal dictionary – see Chapter 5.

Mnemonics

Mnemonics are memory aids, usually using initials or word associations. For example:

The denominator is downstairs $3/4$

to remind you that the lower half of a fraction is called the *denominator*.

You could also use some of the ideas for mnemonics given in Chapter 10.

Personalized ready reckoner

In your work or studies you may have to use the same processes regularly. To save looking these up, have your own 'ready reckoner' for things you often need. For example: 80km ≈ 50 miles; 1" ≈ 2½ cm (the ≈ symbol means 'approximately equal to').

Squared paper

Squared paper helps with 'place value' – keeping your calculations in lines and columns so that the 'units', 'tens' etc. appear in the same columns. You are much less likely to lose figures and your work will look neat. It also helps to form symbols by giving you a square in which to draw them. If you are working with decimal points, it keeps those in the correct place.

Tables or multiplication squares

Multiplication tables can be difficult or impossible for dyslexic people to learn by rote in the conventional way. You can carry a folded tables square in your bag or pocket for reference – see Figure 9.4.

If you want to know what 7 x 8 is, then look along the 7th row to where it crosses the 8th column and you have the answer – 56! To print a copy of this square, please refer to printable document **5** on our online resource.

0	1	2	3	4	5	6	7	8	9	10	11	12
1	1	2	3	4	5	6	7	8	9	10	11	12
2	2	4	6	8	10	12	14	16	18	20	22	24
3	3	6	9	12	15	18	21	24	27	30	33	36
4	4	8	12	16	20	24	28	32	36	40	44	48
5	5	10	15	20	25	30	35	40	45	50	55	60
6	6	12	18	24	30	36	42	48	54	60	66	72
7	7	14	21	28	35	42	49	56	63	70	77	84
8	8	16	24	32	40	48	56	64	72	80	88	96
9	9	18	27	36	45	54	63	72	81	90	99	108
10	10	20	30	40	50	60	70	80	90	100	110	120
11	11	22	33	44	55	66	77	88	99	110	121	132
12	12	24	36	48	60	72	84	96	108	120	132	144

Figure 9.4 Tables square

When you see tables set out like this you can begin to see patterns. There's more about this on our online resource in the *Numbers* section.

You may find the Gypsy method of multiplying useful. This is where you number your fingers and use them to multiply the digits that fall between 6 and 10. This is explained fully in the *Numbers* section of our online resource.

Verbalization

This means saying things aloud or 'hearing' the sound in your head if you are in a place where you can't or don't want to be heard.

- Say it out loud, tracking each figure with your finger as you go. Using your visual and auditory senses, and to some extent your touch as well, can straighten out numbers that bewilder the eye alone: 1066, for example, is easily confused with 1099, 1660, 1990, 6601.
- Say the words for symbols aloud. It helps to remember them.
- If you are a student and need to remember equations and formulas, try saying them in words. For example for the formula: $F = ma$, you say:

    'Force *equals* mass of the object *times* its acceleration.'

    So, remember the words if you find it difficult to remember the formula. But, note, the best thing about formulas is that you don't have to remember the spelling of the words!

When saying something out loud, you can also record it so that you can play it back to learn or identify errors.

Visual enhancement

- Make easily confusable numbers like 6 and 9 different in some way.
- Make symbols memorable in a visual way:

    < means 'less than' and looks like a slightly tilted '**L**' standing for **L**ess than.

- Enlarge the decimal point: 342.10.
- You can use colour in number work as well as with words. For example, you can group maths words together that have the same meaning – using the same colour. Taking the example in Figure 9.2,

each of the four sets of words and symbols would be a different colour (refer to the *Numbers* section of our online resource). This will help you to remember which ones are closely linked.

Visualization

Remember three-dimensional shapes by linking with a familiar object: a sphere looks like an orange; a cylinder is like a beer can. Visualization can also help you to remember numbers. For example, imagine each digit printed on the jars on your kitchen shelf or the side of carriages on a train.

For more examples of strategies refer to the *Numbers* section of our online resource.

Do we all approach maths in the same way?

The answer to this is 'no'. There are two main types of approach to maths that author and lecturer Steve Chinn describes as the inchworm and the grasshopper.

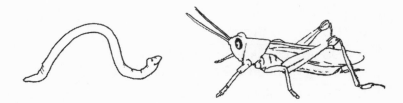

The inchworm represents the type of person who takes a stepwise approach, i.e. by deduction.

The grasshopper, on the other hand, tackles problems in an intuitive way, coming up with the answers but is not necessarily able to explain how.

But in reality, the world isn't made up of inchworms and grasshoppers. We all tend to be a bit of both and use one of the two approaches depending on the situation: hopefully, we choose the one that best suits us for the task in hand. If you are having difficulties with something mathematical, ask yourself whether you are acting like the inchworm or the grasshopper – and then try an approach that the other one would use. It just might help. The following activity will help you to discover whether you are predominantly an inchworm or a grasshopper.

 ACTIVITY 20
What is your main approach to maths?

Answer either yes or no to the questions below. If your answer is 'sometimes', then think what you prefer to do.

		Yes	No
1	Do you pay attention to detail?		
2	Do you use formulas or recipes?		
3	Do you do things in order?		
4	Do you check your answers by going through the sum again?		
5	Do you estimate calculations?		
6	Do you work back from your answer to check?		
7	Do you adjust numbers to make the calculation easier?		
8	Do you do some calculations in your head?		

Figure 9.5 Are you an inchworm or a grasshopper?

If most of your answers are in the shaded boxes then you are probably an inchworm. If most of your answers are in the unshaded boxes, then you are probably a grasshopper. Perhaps you're a bit of both. Good mathematicians tend to use both approaches – choosing the right one suitable for the particular task. This activity has given you a chance to think about the way you do things generally.

If you are predominantly a grasshopper, perhaps you were taught in a class of inchworms by a predominantly inchworm teacher. Being taught by inchworms can be bad news for grasshoppers. Sometimes we don't or can't seem to set out the calculations in the way we were taught, but we still come up with the right answer. Our work may be marked as wrong or heavily corrected. This can lead to a loss of confidence and probably a dislike of maths.

Postscript

> *I have absolutely no problems understanding quite difficult maths: algebra, vectors, calculus. But I used to make mistakes in calculations because my work was so messy and I lost marks. Now, at work I do everything using Excel, Mathcad or squared paper and this stops me making a lot of errors.*

It seems to be OK to admit to 'being no good at maths', more so than admitting that you have writing or spelling difficulties. Most dyslexic difficulties create errors in decoding and doing things in the right order. Many dyslexic people have the ability to understand mathematical concepts and have outstanding creative and spatial abilities.

In this chapter

In this chapter we have looked at:

- the type of difficulties that dyslexic people have with numbers;
- some ideas and strategies for handling numbers;
- our approaches to maths: inchworm and grasshopper.

10
Making memory work for you

Remember remember the fifth of November . . .

Because of this rhyme, most people can remember that Guy Fawkes tried to blow up Parliament on 5th November. But it doesn't help them to remember which year!

In this chapter we will look at memory – how it works and how you can make it work to your advantage.

Short-term and long-term memory

Working memory

Working memory is often called 'short-term memory' but it isn't quite the same. Working memory includes short-term memory – the ability to hold a reasonable amount of information. But it also includes the processing of that information too – the brain handling small chunks of information and putting them together for a purpose. To understand a sentence you have to remember the beginning until you get to the end, so that you can put it all together and make sense of it. At the same time, your brain has to cope with many other demands such as decoding the words, interruptions, poor print, background noise and new words.

Similarly, when doing a mental calculation, you have to remember the original part while you are working out the calculation. For example, if you are calculating 100 minus 88, you have to keep remembering the 100 and the 88, take 8 from 0 which means remembering to borrow 1, then take 9 from 10 and remember that you already have two units. The answer is 12.

It's amazing how our working memory copes!

However, once the sentence is understood, or the answer calculated, we usually forget the original bits of information – the words or the numbers.

Long-term memory

This is the memory we are usually referring to when we talk about 'memory'. It represents information that is stored for long periods of time. Remembering your name, where you went to primary school, where you went on holiday last year – all these need your long-term memory.

There are two types of long-term memory:
- Episodic – remembering a particular incident such as a visit to the cinema last week.
- Semantic – remembering the meaning of a word or the name of a particular object.

'I know I put it in a safe place!'

Remembering is not forgetting

What about forgetting?
- We forget most of what we see, hear or experience within a few seconds! Some pieces of information stick in our minds for much longer.
- Interruptions are really bad news, particularly for dyslexic people. If you are interrupted you will probably lose a substantial part of what you are trying to remember. The thread is broken – it's gone!
- 'Use it or lose it.' For example: A group who took part in a resuscitation course could only recall 15 per cent of the information after 12 months because they hadn't used their new skills.

Why don't I forget how to ride a bike after 20 years?

The actions have become automatic – one action cues the next.

Remembering is about being able to get to the information

Getting at the information we've stored away is called 'recall' or 'retrieval'. All the ideas that we introduce in this chapter will help you to store the information in your brain so that it can be recalled or retrieved when you need it. How often have you said 'it's on the tip of my tongue' or 'I know I saw it in the middle of a page'? These are 'cues' but they are not strong enough to retrieve the information. We usually need more than one cue or association for efficient recall.

Each time you recall something, the pathways in your brain that access that information become better established. It's like the footpath across a field of fully grown corn. It's hard work for the first person to hack their way across it – but once three or four people have walked that way, the path is easier and clearer. So go over things that you want to remember several times. Check them out regularly. Use them. Keep the pathways in your brain open.

What helps you to remember?

You need to make a conscious effort to get information to stick in your brain. Figure 10.1 gives a list of possible things you might want to remember and some suggestions to help.

 ACTIVITY 21
How do you remember?

How might you remember the following?
a) The cash point PIN.
b) The route to somewhere you don't go very often.
c) Where you put a particular book.
d) Important information.

Here are some strategies you could use:
a) Maybe you saw the number in your mind; perhaps you wrote it down on your hand and then copied it onto a piece of paper.
b) For the route – you might have visualized it in your mind or imagined a map. You might have drawn it using symbols for distinctive landmarks such as the church on the corner.
c) You may keep all your books in topic groups.
d) You may remember information you need by putting it all in one place, perhaps in a file marked with the title so you can find it easily.

Improving your memory

Encoding

When we talk about how to 'improve' memory, we are usually talking about **encoding** more efficiently so that we get something into our long-term memory and

Things to remember	How you might do it	Type of strategy
Names	Imagine the face on a poster with the name written below it.	Visual
Phrases for using in a foreign country	At home, imagine yourself in various situations in which you have to use these phrases – use them.	Doing/ acting
Numbers	Group them rhythmically – grouping in 3s works best as it seems to reduce the tendency to recall them in the wrong order.	Auditory
	Speak them aloud – don't just read them to yourself. Articulating and hearing the sounds of the numbers registers them in your auditory and visual short-term memory.	Auditory/ visual
Where you left something – a spatial orientation problem such as finding your car in a car park	Find landmarks to link to – such as the direction of a nearby church or prominent tree.	Visual

Figure 10.1 Some memory strategies

improve the way we retrieve it. We are imprinting it in our brain in such a way that our brain can recognize it when we want to access it.

Note: we're going to use the word 'encoding' a lot. It is a useful technical word and it means the way we get our brains to interact with the information in our working memory so that we can store it in our long-term memory.

It's a myth that memory gets worse with age. Our memories do fill up as the years pass, adding vast numbers of experiences. Imagine more and more things piled untidily in a heap – like a pile of unsorted washing – and you can see that it can get harder and harder to 'sort' and 'retrieve' as the pile grows. If you sort by colour, for example into separate piles, it will be quicker to find a particular garment. The same is true in your memory. You really can improve your memory – this means improving the way you store and retrieve information. It is not as if you are actually 'losing' things – it is more a case that you cannot remember where you put them.

> *The person who thinks over his experiences most and weaves them into systematic relations with each other will be the one with the best memory.*
> (William James, psychologist and philosopher)

Here are 13 suggestions – the 13 Ms – to make things more retrievable. Those marked * are discussed in more detail below.
- Make sense of it – it's very hard to remember something you don't understand.
- Make it stick* – we remember things that we are interested in.
- Make it memorable* – we remember things that are unusual or exaggerated.

- Make it multi-sensory* – see it, touch it, hear it, do it, smell it.
- Make use of your memory style – bright colour, rhyming words, acting it out (refer back to your learning style activity in Chapter 3).
- Make it organized* – into groups, patterns, categories.
- Make it into chunks* – a few things at a time, about 5 chunks work best.
- Make time for review – without reviewing what we have learned we tend to forget much of it after 24 hours.
- Make a mnemonic* – build links to things you can remember.

- Make a mind map – see the *Writing* section on our online resource.
- Make the best time and place for memory work*.
- Make links – to things you already understand.
- Make time to practise – recall improves the retrieval pathways.

Now let's look at some of these suggestions in a bit more detail.

Making it stick

To make it stick, you need to:

PAY ATTENTION *and* PROCESS ACTIVELY

Pay attention:	Process actively:
Sit up, get ready for action, be aware of what needs doing, concentrate, clear the mind of other things	Use your strengths, make links, make it multi-sensory, apply some of the 13 Ms

When you meet a person for the first time you usually concentrate on making conversation. Try repeating their name as they say it: Say 'Hello Jim'. Then, during the conversation with Jim include his name several times: 'Do you live near here Jim?' 'Jim, what do you think of . . .' etc. You might say some of these silently! This will help you to recall his name next time you meet.

It also helps to link the person's name with some visual characteristic. For example, if Jim has reddish hair you can say to yourself: 'he is Jim the red' and so store his name in your memory.

You are **paying attention**:

Listening for Jim's name, looking for his visual characteristics.

. . . and **processing actively**:

Using his name several times, linking his name to his hair colour.

Making it memorable

Some ideas to make things memorable include: exaggerating the size, the shape and the sound of whatever you are trying to remember; imagining it as massive – writing it out in huge letters; making it more colourful.

Making it multi-sensory

When you are trying to remember something important, make it multi-sensory, a strategy we've mentioned several times in previous chapters. We remember something even better when we use more than one of our senses. This is called *enriched* encoding, i.e. we are using more routes in our brain to recall something.

The more ways the whole experience is encoded, the more your memory will be triggered, helping you to remember and recall things. We call this multi-sensory learning – learning using many senses.

Imprinting memory in your brain in a multi-sensory way can happen subconsciously. For example, the memory of a visit to the seaside can be awakened by the smell of the sea; the feel of the sand through your toes; the sight of the waves with their breakers; the sound of seagulls. You can recall all this without having tried to learn it. So using more than one of your senses deliberately can be very powerful. Figure 10.2 gives some ideas and strategies using different senses.

Where possible, combine more than one idea from each section to make it multi-sensory. For example, to remember how to use a new piece of equipment:

- make a diagram numbered in the order you need to do things; AND
- act out using the equipment in spare moments; AND
- say the operations out loud as you act them out.

Making it organized

Put information you regularly confuse into categories that emphasize the differences and make it distinctive.

Our memory is a bit like a library. A disorganized memory would be like a library where all the books have just been placed on the shelves in any old order. Libraries arrange books in subject order and then in alphabetical order of the author's surname. This makes it easier to find a book. The same thing applies to your memory. Organizing things you need to learn gives a structure and pattern to them and makes things easier to recall.

Make it into chunks

Your short-term memory can handle information and get it into long-term memory better if what you are trying to learn is broken down into manageable chunks. Chunking is an excellent strategy for dyslexics. Here are some ways to chunk information:

Using visual memory – working through seeing

- Use colour – highlight words, colour things in.
- Draw it – make an attractive poster, diagram, spider diagram or mind map.
- Adapt a diagram from a book and make it colourful.
- Use semi-sticky notes in different colours and stick them up round the house.
- Try memory videos – details in the *Memory* section of our online resource.

Using auditory memory – working through hearing

- Record the information and play it back several times . . . *while washing up, travelling, or relaxing.*
- Repeat things aloud to yourself as if you were explaining it to someone.
- Discuss it with someone.
- Work with music in the background – *experiment with different kinds of music.*

Using kinaesthetic memory – working through doing, touching, smelling

- Act it out – make a story.
- Interact with the information – *ask questions, make notes, diagrams or drawings*
- Put information on index cards that you can pull out of your pocket every time you have a spare moment.
- Walk about while learning.
- Take regular breaks and do something physical in them.
- Try things out or imagine doing them.

Figure 10.2 Ideas and strategies using different senses

- Chop long words into smaller words or syllables to learn the spelling.
- Pick out key words and just try to remember those.
- Separate things out visually – use space.
- Don't spend too long on any learning task without taking breaks.

Using mnemonics

Any method that helps you to remember, often a rhyme, is called a mnemonic (pronounced *ne-mon-ic).*

> *In fourteen hundred and ninety-two*
> *Columbus sailed the ocean blue* (and discovered America).

The variation likely to suit most dyslexic people is called 'location mnemonics' because it uses seeing and doing strategies.

Location mnemonics

- First choose a location that is very familiar to you, such as your home and garden, or the town where you live.
- Walk around your chosen area regularly in the same sequence, whether or not you have something to learn. Look carefully at it all – imprint it on your memory.
- Try imagining it with your eyes shut until you 'see' it just as if you were there.
- Now look at whatever it is you need to remember.
- 'Walk' through your location in your mind using the route you always take and link everything you need to remember to things on your route.
- You can make it even more vivid by weaving a story. Then, all you have to do is walk around or imagine your route and many, if not all, the things you want to remember will pop into your mind. Location mnemonics work because we remember

the location better than unconnected or loosely connected facts.

Other types of mnemonics include:
- number-rhyme;
- memory videos.

These would suit those who are better at remembering words and sounds. See the *Memory* section in our online resource.

 ACTIVITY 22
Try the location mnemonics strategy

Try using the instructions for location mnemonics given above to learn something that would be useful for you to be able to remember.

Repetition

Repeating something that we want to remember many times can be useful if it is simple or short term. You could even chant it to a familiar tune.

Making links

To help us remember complex information we can make links to things we already know – something that is already firmly anchored in our memory. We need to understand it and put it in context.

It's like a series of boats all moored together with their ropes to the dock. The boats represent the new information; the dock is our existing memory. So you relate new material as closely and as richly as you can to your own interests and previous knowledge.

Making the best time and place for memory work

Time

There are certain times and places that are better for memorizing things.
- Some people are better in the mornings, others later in the day. Experiment with different times to find which is best for you.

- There is evidence to suggest that we remember things we learn or do just before going to bed. On the other hand, we don't take in things very well if we are tired. There is a balance to be struck here!
- Be aware that we don't learn well if we are upset, concerned or in a state of panic.

Place

Find a good place to work in. Avoid distractions, especially visual ones. Background music of the right kind can be helpful in filtering out distracting sounds. Remember you need a comfortable temperature, a comfortable seating position and good light.

Pause for a moment

Commitment and enthusiasm are the most important aspects of the ability to remember and recall things. A schoolboy remembers all the names of his football heroes. So put some enthusiasm into what you are doing. Set yourself short-term aims – break the task into smaller ones and reward yourself in some way for achieving each. If you were trying to help someone else to remember and learn, you would reward and praise at each stage, almost without thinking. So do it for yourself too!

> *I have to learn the Highway Code by next Friday for my written test. I will go through it all by Wednesday and then open a bottle of wine!*

Other ideas

You will find other memory ideas in Chapter 7, which is about organization, and details about technology that can aid your memory in Chapter 11.

Improving memory by diet, supplements and exercise

Memory is definitely improved when our general health is good, so eat a balanced diet and take regular exercise. A balanced diet means plenty of fresh fruit and vegetables, a reasonable amount of protein, not too much starchy food, very little sugar and salt. Avoid fast foods that are generally too fatty. Keep within the guidelines with alcohol as too much has a detrimental effect on memory. There is some evidence that fish oils help in brain functioning so eat plenty of oily fish such as herring, sardines, salmon, etc.

There is a definite relationship between exercise and learning – it really pays to take a break from brain work. A brisk 10-minute walk round the block or up and down the stairs will get you working more effectively than a quick sugar snack, because exercise releases endorphins in the brain. You will then be more alert and your memory will work better too.

Many people have found that Brain Gym® helps with memory and learning. It offers particular activities and movement sequences to improve your learning ability. You can find more information on their website (www.braingym.org). If you think it might help you, give it a try. Ask around – you may find someone who has experience of it. It is used a lot with children although it does also seem to work for many adults.

ACTIVITY 23
What do you need to remember?

Jot down the main things you would like to be able to remember better.

You may find that things fall into different groups. You may have a list of 'facts' such as names, numbers, locations of objects, and a different list of more complicated ideas – notes for a report etc.

What strategies will you try? Jot down a list of any ideas in this chapter that you would like to try or any ideas that have been triggered in your mind by reading this. Keep the list in a safe place ready for when you next need to remember something.

In this chapter

In this chapter we've looked at:
- short- and long-term memory;
- how we best remember things;
- how you can improve memory and recall;
- a range of ideas and strategies to help remember things.

PART 3

Resources for you

In this part there are two chapters and four appendices that give details of resources, books and contacts that you might find useful.

- Chapter 11
  Helping yourself with technology
  Hardware and software packages and other resources

- Chapter 12
  Looking wider
  Education, the workplace and organizations

11

Helping yourself with technology

There is no doubt that most dyslexics find that computers give them a huge amount of independence. Technical solutions of all kinds can help dyslexics with reading, writing, spelling, grammar and organization. In this chapter you can find medium and high tech ideas to help you.

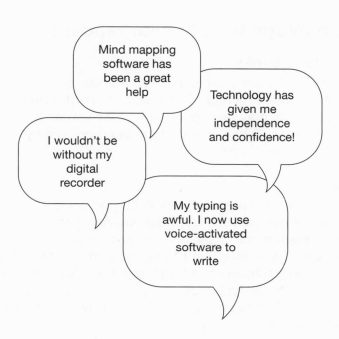

Finding your way around this chapter

We hope you will find this chapter informative even if you are wary of technology. It summarizes the resources that are currently available (prices quoted are approximate at the time of going to press). We hope it will help you to think about what would be useful. Figure 11.1 may help you to find what you want.

We have grouped technical solutions according to the tasks that you may want to do. There are many low cost solutions too – items that have been around for a very long time such as paper, pens, pencils, card, wood etc. or made from such materials. Many of these solutions, often simple gadgets such as colour coding, charts and removable sticky notes, have already been discussed in previous chapters. We have included a list at the end of this chapter.

Technology to help with reading

Recorded books

A lot of books are available as recordings, often edited to cut down their length. If you want to read a book for pleasure, this may be a good option for you as listening can be easier. E-books are becoming more widely available – see below.

E-books

These are in digital format which can be bought over the counter or downloaded from the internet. They can be read through a computer or there are a number of dedicated, book-sized and therefore portable devices, some of which have useful features. Look for one where you can alter the font, size and colour. If you want to listen as well as read, look for one that has a read-back facility with headphones.

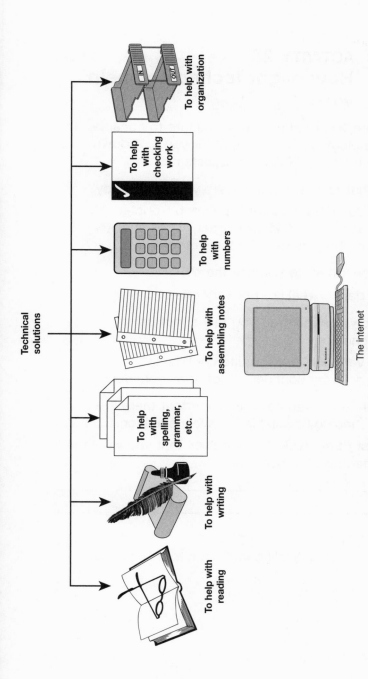

Figure 11.1 Technical solutions discussed in this chapter
(There is more information about the internet, useful websites, software and hardware on our online resource.)

Technical solutions

To help with reading

To help with writing

To help with spelling, grammar, etc.

To help with assembling notes

To help with numbers

To help with checking work

To help with organization

The internet

ACTIVITY 23

How might technology help you?

Before you read on, take a minute to consider how technology could be useful for you. Jot down your answers to the following questions.

- What technical items have you got already?

  computer   laptop   palmtop   printer
  scanner   digital recorder   spell checker
  mobile phone   iPhone   other

- How often do you use them?

  daily   weekly   not very often   never

- How confident do you feel about using technology?

  very confident   quite confident
  not very confident   not at all confident

- Whatever you have, imagine that there is technology available for every situation.

  List three dyslexic difficulties that you would like a technical remedy for.

  1 _____

  2 _____

  3 _____

Now read on. We'll come back to this exercise later.

Using the standard software on your computer

Many documents at work or at college may be available as electronic files. With a computer you can adapt and use them to overcome some of your own dyslexic difficulties. You can:

- change the typeface (font) and the size of the letters;
- change the colour of the letters and of the background;
- alter the colours and fonts you see on your screen;
- copy extracts from the text;
- add your own notes to the text.

So it's worth asking whether you can have any document as a Word file.

Speech output – text reader – text to speech

These are all terms used for the same thing. All modern computers are multi-media so, with appropriate software, your computer can read the text out as it appears on the screen. The synthesized speech has improved over the years and is now easier to listen to and can often be adapted to suit your preferences. Look out for developments such as using a smart phone with optical character reader (OCR) software that can read any text back to you.

Speech output can be useful in the same way as recordings and talking books are. It helps with:

- comprehension and concentration;
- pronunciation of new and unfamiliar words;
- skim-reading;
- proofreading your own work.

Take time to consider which package is best for you –
some are definitely not useful for dyslexic people.
Check the following. Does it:

- highlight the word as it reads it?
- allow you to choose it to read back by word,
  sentence or paragraph?
- offer alternatives to what you have written in case
  you've got it wrong?

Costs vary, but the range is approximately £160–£370.
Some basic free software is available. Specialist advice
is essential (see Appendix C) before spending money.

Reading pens

A reading pen is a miniature scanner, about the size of a
chunky pen but easier to hold. There are various types
available, they all have a synthesized voice and can be
used with an ear-piece. They read out individual words
and can give their definitions. They might not recognize
some subject-specific words but specialized content is
available as an extra as are various languages. Prices
are quite high (£200). There are similar devices for
scanning small extracts of text – e.g. quotations and
things you want to remember – and you can also load
the text onto your computer later. These are useful if you
do not have immediate access to a computer.

Scanners

If you want to read something by listening to it, and it
isn't available as a recording or an electronic file, a
scanner might be worth having. It's a hand-held or
flat-bed device (something like a photocopier) that
copies the text and converts it to a word-processed
document. You can then adapt and use that in all the
ways we've already suggested. The software that
converts the image to text sometimes has problems
when presented with unclear print, symbols or complex
layouts. However, such packages are getting more

sophisticated and some can even read handwriting. Cost – £60 upwards plus the OCR software (£80). Watch out for new developments.

Coloured light

If you have found coloured overlays helpful (see Chapter 5) you may like to use a lamp with a coloured bulb. There is also a useful but expensive lamp that allows you to change the colour through the whole spectrum to suit you and the conditions (£300).

Technology to help with writing – getting the ideas down

Many dyslexic people are articulate and express themselves well verbally. Slow writing, lack of confidence with spelling or grammar and other difficulties can interfere with the flow of ideas. Technology can help by separating the 'transcription' skills from the 'composition' – the creative ideas and structure (as described in Chapter 6).

Digital recorders

Dictating can remove many of the difficulties of 'transcription' (see Chapter 6). You can dictate your ideas into a recorder, play it back and type the ideas into your word processor like an audio-typist. You can use your word processor to correct and edit your text. They are mobile phone sized, so easy to carry around. Cost: from very cheap to £130+ for a sophisticated digital recorder – check that the key features include indexing. Some mobile phones have basic recording features. If you dislike hearing your own voice on a recorder, you can get used to it by putting a finger in one ear while you are recording.

Coloured light

See the reading section above.

Standard word processors

Set up your word processor so that your text is as easy as possible for you to read. Ensure your screen is free from reflections and adjust its brightness and contrast. Take some time to check up on your word-processing skills. Some choices you can make within standard word processor packages are:

- The colour of the text and the background.
- The shape and size of the letters. You can use the zoom facility to display the text on your screen in your preferred size.
- Make your text left-justified (as in this book). This helps you to track the text across and down the page, and avoids awkward spacing between letters.
- Set up the AutoCorrect facility to correct errors you're particularly likely to make and to complete words and phrases you type in frequently.
- Add commonly used commands to the toolbar, to avoid hunting through menus.
- Use key strokes to reduce the number of times you use the mouse (e.g. *Control B* gives you bold).
- Learn how to use Style Sheets so that you can use Outline mode to see the structure of your document and change it easily.
- Create a template if you're going to produce several documents of a similar kind.
- Be sure to save your work frequently – every five minutes.

If you want to find out more about these facilities, use the Help menu. You might want to look for an IT course at your local college. They are often inexpensive and sometimes free. The *Abilitynet* website has some downloadable information sheets. Note that, for academic writing, there is some useful software available for doing referencing and footnotes.

Touch typing

It is very useful to be able to touch type – to know which fingers hit which keys so that you can type without looking at the keyboard. We recommend that you should try to learn this skill as the brain doesn't then have to think about the letters as you type – it becomes automatic. There are a number of software packages for learning to type (£20–£40) or you may find a local college course.

Voice recognition software

Packages that fall into this group allow you to talk directly to your computer, which then transcribes your speech into word-processed text. You may have trouble if your speech isn't particularly clear or varies a lot. You'll need training, and so will your computer – it has to learn to recognize *your* voice. This may mean several hours of work. You'll probably need to weigh up the effort required against the degree of difficulty you have with spelling and expressing yourself in writing. Many voice-recognition software packages are available at affordable prices (£50–£500). Seek advice from a specialist and buy the best you can afford. Before you buy anything, try it out. We recommend developing dictating skills with a digital recorder first. If you decide to buy the software we suggest that a USB connecting headset will give you better service.

Technology to help with words – spelling, grammar etc.

You might want to check a spelling, the meaning of a word, or find the right word to use. Difficulties with reading and alphabetical order can make using a dictionary hard work, if not impossible. Technology can help.

Spelling

There are a number of hand-held spell checkers available (from £25). Some include definitions (as in a dictionary) and some include a thesaurus that will offer you alternative words you can use. The pitfalls of using any type of spell checker are mentioned in the section on computers below. It is much quicker to use these electronic devices than paper-based ones and they are more portable than a computer. But don't get anything too small because it will be difficult to read. If you are a student and intend buying a small, portable spell checker to use it in exams, make sure that the one you choose will be permitted.

Spelling and grammar checkers

Standard word processors offer some help with spelling and grammar. Some packages provide help with words that are spelled differently but sound the same (homophones such as 'hear' and 'here') by giving you an idea of the meaning.

Some software will highlight or even correct mistakes as you type. If you find that these interruptions interfere with the flow of your ideas, you can alter the default settings so that the checks are not made automatically. You can run the check when you are ready. Make sure that your language setting is correct: UK English for most English-speaking countries, US English for North America. The default setting is often US English – change the setting to the one you need.

Spell checkers are useful, but they cannot be relied on completely. They cannot distinguish a misspelled word if the misspelling is itself a word. If you mistyped 'boat' as 'beat' or if you type 'their' instead of 'there', the spell checker will not recognize an error has been made. More advanced packages will identify some of these and ask which word you mean by giving you a selection. If you're concerned about spelling, consider purchasing speech output software because hearing the wrong word can help you to see the mistake.

You can run the standard grammar checker through when you have finished. Bear in mind that some of the comments you get are not particularly helpful. One grammar checker, for example, questions whether you should be using 'that' instead of 'which'. But if you type

They was going out

it will query: *'subject – verb agreement?'* The word 'was' will be highlighted and it will suggest using 'were'. This can be very useful if your grammar is a bit wobbly.

Predictive software

Predictive software is a facility that offers you a choice of words. Several packages include a predictive facility. When you type the first few letters of a word, a list will be displayed of the words you use most often starting with those letters. Click on the one you want and it will be inserted for you. For example, if you type 'psy' you might get this list:

- psychology
- psychologist
- psychiatry
- psychoanalyst

The more letters you can type in, the more likely the word you want will be included in the selection. The software remembers how often and how recently you've used the words it comes up with, and lists the most likely ones at the top. You can also add words to its memory but you must ensure that they are spelled correctly.

Meaning

Good dictionaries are available on CD-ROM. If you type a word or highlight it in the text you're reading or writing,

you can use the dictionary to give you the full definition
or even check the pronunciation. There are some useful
dictionaries freely available on the internet – check
whether they are UK or US spellings.

Finding the right word or another word

A thesaurus is a dictionary of synonyms – words or
phrases that have the same or similar meaning. It is
useful for finding a more appropriate word, or finding an
alternative when you have used a particular word too
often. A thesaurus will help you to increase your
vocabulary and improve the quality of your written work.
Some word processors include one, but, like
dictionaries, it is possible to buy an excellent thesaurus
on CD-ROM or the internet.

Technology to help with making notes

Making notes usually means doing several tasks at the
same time – listening or reading, understanding,
summarizing, writing. This can be difficult if you're
dyslexic, but technology can help. For example, you may
be able to use your mobile phone to record your notes
or photograph the parts you want to refer to.

Recorders

Recorders have improved with the advances in digital
technology so get the best you can afford. You can do
a lot with the basic cassette recorder that has been
around since the 1960s if you have one, but digital
recorders have many additional facilities. You can edit
the recording and they provide many hours of recording
space. They are also small and easy to carry around.
With agreement of others involved, you could record
meetings, talks or lectures and make notes from your
recordings. You can also record your notes at the time –
it's better than recording everything.

Digital recorders are very versatile. You can use them with voice recognition software when you return to your computer. You might find that more convenient than lugging a laptop around with you.

Portable keyboards

These are robust keyboards (not laptops) with a built-in carrying handle and a reasonable amount of memory. They are light, relatively inexpensive (from £110) and have very basic word processing facilities. You can take them anywhere – they have rechargeable batteries – and you can transfer what you have written to your computer when you get home. They can be used, however, without a computer.

Laptop and hand-held computers

Many people use a laptop as their main computer these days but remember that they are easier to damage or get stolen when carried around.

There are a number of smaller hand-held products available – you may know them as 'smart phones', 'PDAs', 'netbooks' or 'palmtops'. Though more restricted in facilities, these devices can be very useful, particularly when used in association with a computer. They are small, very portable and can be kept in a pocket. They can be set up to remind you of important things and other useful organizing options; you can make readable notes; some have recording facilities and they can be synchronized with your computer. Advances in design have overcome some of the initial problems associated with their size. There is a range of more advanced software ('apps') that can be added if you need it.

Technology to help with numbers

Most modern telephones and mobiles can store numbers you use frequently and many have basic calculators. There are many calculators on the market, including ones that talk (try the RNIB for information). Don't buy one that is more complicated than you need.

Most computers have a calculator package installed. In addition, they all come with spreadsheets such as Excel, which can help with calculations, keeping accounts etc. They keep figures in columns and lines, which is often a difficulty when doing calculations. *Verdana* is a good font to use with spreadsheets as the numbers are clear. There are various maths packages available. We recommend taking a course for using spreadsheets at your local college to find out more about these versatile packages.

Technology to help with checking your work

Much of the technology we have mentioned so far is also useful for checking your work. We have summarized this in Figure 11.2. Work produced on a word processor package is neat and easier to check.

I changed the settings on my computer to make my screen easier to read. This way, I can spot my mistakes easily.

Technology to help with organization

There are various inexpensive ways to help with organization:

- A pocket-sized electronic organizer has many facilities for storing information, telephone numbers, addresses, dates – and it will remind you of appointments.
- Many mobile phones have similar features.

Things to check	Technology to use
Have I used the correct word?	• Reading pen. • Text reader. • Thesaurus or dictionary software.
Is my grammar correct?	• Digital recorder: record as you read aloud, then listen. • Speech output/text reader. • Grammar checker.
Have I said what I wanted to say?	• Digital recorder: record as you read aloud, then listen. • Speech output/text reader.
Is the punctuation correct?	• Digital recorder: record as you read aloud, then listen. • Speech output/text reader.
Have I spelled the word correctly?	• Spell checkers. • Speech output/text reader.
General proof-reading	• Use the zoom facility to enlarge the print to 150. Mistakes can show up best like this.

Figure 11.2 Summary of technology to use when checking work

Software

Many computers come with software to help with organization so check this out first. Software packages designed to help you to organize your ideas are sometimes based on mind maps; others draw flow diagrams or allow you to brainstorm, sort and order your ideas in a choice of formats (look for 'concept mapping' software, prices from £60). New products are always coming onto the market, so we suggest that you discuss your needs with an assistive technology specialist such as a needs assessor or access to work adviser. Most packages have free 'tasters' that you can download from the internet.

More on technology

Printers

If you have a computer or a portable keyboard, you will need a printer. Get the best you can afford – make colour a priority. Throughout this book we have mentioned how useful it is to work using colour. If you are using any of the standard or specialist packages to produce work you will want to print it out in colour. Ink cartridges are expensive, so find the most economical way of printing:

- Try to get into the habit of reading as much as you can on screen by altering the font, changing the background colour and using the zoom facility to increase the size, to make it comfortable.
- Print out in draft quality only, until you are sure your work is complete and error free.
- Don't print out everything from the internet – you often get pages of things you don't want. Either copy and paste into a Word file and then edit, or save the internet (html) file in a folder on your computer.

Useful software

New packages are appearing all the time. Again the advice is, don't rush out and buy something. Here are some things you can do first:

- Consider carefully what your needs are and what you really want to do. The activities at the start and end of this chapter give you time to think about this.

- Ask other users what they find helpful – ask them to show you or let you try it. Ask them what works and what might be frustrating about the package. Don't try to copy their software – this is illegal.
- Look for sample packages to download from the internet to try out.
- Contact a specialist – see Appendix C for organizations that can advise you. If you are in work, including being self-employed, you can get advice through the Access to Work Scheme. If you are a student then you have a right to a needs assessment.
- Don't buy everything at once because it takes time to learn a new software package. Make sure you have time to get to grips with it – build learning time into your weekly diary.

The internet

The internet will give you access to a vast amount of information, advice, dictionaries, encyclopaedias, reference works and websites of every kind. Check the source – you can usually depend on internet addresses containing: .ac, .edu, .org, .bbc, .gov. Be aware, many websites go out of date quite quickly. You may have no way of assessing their quality, but don't be put off – use the internet intelligently, just as you would a library. If you find a site that you'd like to return to, add it to your Favourites or Bookmarks. We have listed some *useful links* on the website. *The Rough Guide to the Internet* (available in all major bookshops) is a very useful pocket-sized book that is frequently updated. We recommend you buy a copy if you have reservations about using the internet. Make sure you get the most recent edition. You can find useful tutorials on YouTube while social networking sites can be a helpful source for sharing experience of technology.

What might you need?

✍ ACTIVITY 24
What do I need?

Now look back at your answers to Activity 23 and answer the remaining questions.

If you already have some technology, how can you use it in ways you hadn't thought of before? Note three things that you will try soon:

1 _____

2 _____

3 _____

What ideas have you found for the 3 dyslexic difficulties that you said you would like a technical remedy for in your answers to Activity 23?

1 _____

2 _____

3 _____

Justifying the expense

If you find something that is useful but costly, think whether it could be useful in other ways. For example, would other members of your family find it useful? Would it be useful at work? Your employer may be prepared to purchase some software for you. If you are a student, talk to your needs assessor. Some software licences will allow you to load it onto more than one machine – your home computer, for example.

Getting to grips with technology

Ensure that you get good training to get you started. For more high-tech items such as computers and software, some follow-up training is likely to be essential and, ideally, should be on a one-to-one basis and delivered to meet the dyslexic learning style: multi-sensory and structured. You can't learn everything at once, so start with something that will make the greatest difference for you. Contact your supplier or local college for advice and training.

There is a lot of technology lying around not being used – you may have some yourself. The advice in this chapter may have persuaded you to use it at last. Don't be tempted to rush out and buy – seek some good advice from a specialist supplier (see Appendix C). Talk to others about what they have found useful.

Give yourself time to try out equipment or software. Play with it, explore, experiment at times that are not crucial. Children and young people can be very helpful with this – they are growing up with the new technology! If you buy expensive equipment, don't forget to check whether you have insurance that covers you for loss or damage, including if you take equipment away from home.

Technology has made both my life and work so much easier. It's been worth the extra bit it cost me.

Finally, here is a list of low tech items you might find useful.

Low tech items

We suggest that you keep a supply of these low tech items. Local office suppliers, supermarkets and other shops usually have such items at reasonable prices.
- A4 pad of squared paper for keeping writing neat, for doing calculations or for planning.

- A3 or larger plain pads – such as flip chart pads, or wallpaper lining paper for posters and planning.
- Highlighter pens and felt tips in a range of colours.
- Envelope files in a range of colours.
- Plastic document wallets in a range of colours for filing or for makeshift coloured overlays.
- Document boxes for filing the wallets.
- Pens and pencils of all shapes, sizes and colours – fat, thin, fibre-tipped etc. Marker pens for posters.
- Sticky notes in a range of shapes and colours for brainstorming, memos, etc.
- Coloured page markers (semi-adhesive).
- Index cards for personal dictionary, facts to learn etc.
- Small address book for personal dictionary.
- Coloured file dividers.
- Sticky labels in a range of shapes and colours – good for labelling.
- Scrap books.
- Pack of A4 paper in the tint you find easier to read.
- Tinted card for making bookmarks and tracking rulers.
- Selection of coloured paperclips.
- Save scrap paper for practising writing, testing spelling, making spider diagrams, printing out drafts etc.
- Copy holder – cookery book holder.
- Diary, personal organizer, etc.

In this chapter we've described lots of technology that's available currently. Keep a look out for anything new.

12
Looking wider

. . . the world's my oyster!
(From *The Merry Wives of Windsor* Act 2,
Scene 2 by William Shakespeare)

I showed my
line manager my dyslexia
report and she's been
very helpful in
meeting my needs

Many of my
colleagues just
think dyslexia
means I can't
spell!

This chapter looks at the wider aspects of dyslexia –
we look at help available from other professionals and
organizations. We suggest ways of coping in education,
whether it is for leisure, training at work, further or higher
education. We consider workplace issues and the
resources that are available. The epilogue encourages
you to think about where you go from here.

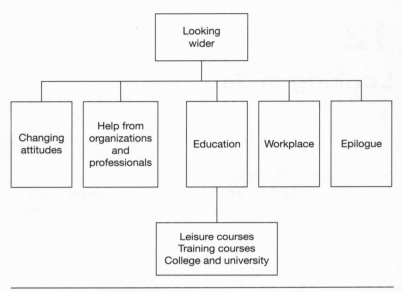

Figure 12.1 Finding your way around this chapter

Help from organizations and professionals

Specialist tuition

One-to-one tuition is available through several organizations and qualified individuals who will have a specialist postgraduate qualification. Some of the professional organizations listed in Appendix C will have a list of appropriate tutors.

Optometrists

In Chapter 5 we mentioned how useful coloured transparent overlays can be with reading – they seem to hold the print still on the page and help to make reading more comfortable. A large proportion of dyslexic people have problems with visual discomfort. If you have tried coloured overlays and found an improvement in comfort with reading, then we suggest that you talk to your optometrist about tinted spectacles.

In fact, we recommend that you see an optometrist if you experience any discomfort: distortion, blurring, headaches, difficulty concentrating when reading. The cause may be to do with the eye and this should be corrected first. If some symptoms still persist, then you can ask your local optician for details of the nearest optometrist who specializes in dyslexia and the use of a piece of equipment called the intuitive colorimeter.

Counselling

It can be enormously helpful to share your feelings about dyslexia with someone who is independent, and who won't judge you. A counsellor's role is to help you to cope more effectively. They can also help you to handle stress and raise self-esteem – see Chapter 8.

Education and learning

Educational providers are often very helpful in offering facilities to meet needs. They are required by law to make reasonable adjustments for disabled people under Part 4 of the Disability Discrimination Act, 1995. Dyslexia is defined as a disability under this Act. It is, therefore, a good idea to check what any educational institution offers in the way of specific support and facilities.

The driving test

It's possible to have extra time to complete the theory part of the test. You will need proof of your dyslexia for this allowance. If you have difficulty distinguishing your left from your right, it is also acceptable during the practical test to ask the examiner to point out the direction to take.

Leisure courses

Leisure courses can be fun and also useful. You might be concerned about signing up for evening or day classes. You are making quite a financial commitment and you may be concerned about what you could be asked to do in the class. Here are some points to consider:

- Choose a course that really interests you.
- Go to a 'taster' session if it is offered.
- Talk to the course organizer beforehand if you have any concerns.

Languages for leisure

If you have had difficulty learning the grammar and spelling of your own language, this may put you off attempting another. But it wasn't learning to *speak* your own language that gave you the problem. So build up your confidence with another language by concentrating on conversation classes at first. You may find that you are really good at speaking but that it's hard to learn the words. It can be difficult to learn a word that you can't see or you don't know how to spell – see Chapter 10 for some memory strategies. All language learners agree that if you don't use it, you lose it – so practise as often as you can.

- Check out classes in your area – some may offer conversation only.
- There are many good language computer packages available that use multi-sensory learning – hearing and seeing at the same time. You can play the lessons over and over.
- Find a native speaker who will speak slowly for you. They are often eager to help and you may also be able to help them with their spoken English. Dyslexic people can often benefit by 'immersion' – living in a foreign country for example.

You are likely to find Italian and Spanish easier than French. Languages like French are harder because their sounds are not always represented by the same letters, and groups of letters do not always sound the same.

This doesn't mean that you shouldn't attempt foreign languages. Getting a feel for speaking the language first will help. Dyslexic difficulties tend to affect all learning in languages and learning music too.

Music

Do you have a good ear for a tune or a good sense of rhythm? Do you want to read music?

There is an increasing body of opinion, backed up by research, which suggests that musical training can improve the ability to hear syllables in words more clearly. This training helps people to develop better awareness of rhythms and stresses. In the language we use for babies, speech rhythm is one of the earliest clues that the infants use to segment speech. This appears to be true across all languages. Music can develop an awareness through the repetition of the 'beat' by simply tapping out the beats heard or played. Music making can also be a very enjoyable way of doing something with other people that brings out creative expression. It also increases confidence whereas books may be less rewarding if there is any difficulty with reading.

Dyslexia can be an asset in music – the creative and holistic skills are useful. But some things can give rise to difficulties so here are a few ideas to help:
- As with other things, make music multi-sensory: yes, hear it, but also feel it and see it too.
- Practise playing an instrument with your eyes shut to help you feel where the notes are.
- Use colour to help you remember the notes on the lines and spaces of the music.
- Apply chunking – learn the notes of music first, then apply the rhythm.
- Keep going when playing. Ignore your mistakes. Record what you are doing and then go back, listen

to it, pick out any mistakes and try to identify what it is that is causing you to make the mistake.
- Try playing (or singing) the difficult bit really slowly until you get it mostly right. Then try increasing the speed until you get it right.
- Look for patterns in music. Learn these and then identify variations.
- Listen to a recording of the piece over and again until it becomes familiar.
- Memorize it using whatever strategies you can devise. Knowing the notes and rhythm well allows you to concentrate on interpretation.
- A useful website with helpful ideas is www.music goals.com/

- Sight reading can be very difficult if you are dyslexic. Look in the *Memory* section of the online resource for an idea that we know has worked for some people.

Teachers can help by:
- Using multi-sensory teaching strategies, for example, to show the *shape* of a triad, the length of notes, clefs in different colours.
- On the manuscript, marking in pencil where the beats fall. It can help to beat out the rhythm first.
- Explaining musical terms in simpler language or making it visual by, for example, drawing a sad face for a passage in a minor key.

- Using wooden 'Beat-blox' devised by Fiona Greaves to understand the rhythms in written music. For more information and how to obtain them, see *Useful links* in the *IT* section on our online resource.

Choosing a course at college or university
Dyslexia presents an additional dimension to your learning. You can consider a number of questions to

help you choose your course such as those we have given below to help you focus on your choice.

- What is your interest in the subject or topic?
- How relevant is it to your career plans?
- Is previous experience or knowledge necessary or useful? E.g. use of statistics.
- Do you need any advice from others?
- Will relevant work experience be useful?
- Are you aware of any demands likely to be difficult for you? E.g. the amount of reading.
- Will the course give you the qualification you want?

Strategies for coping at college or university

Most colleges and universities offer a confidential student support service that will help you:

- get a dyslexia assessment or reassessment;
- apply for additional time in examinations or assignments;
- apply, if appropriate, as early as possible for the Disabled Student Allowance (DSA), which can supply both teaching support and computer technology and software;
- find a mentor, a friendly fellow student with experience of your course.

University libraries are also getting much better at offering guidance in using their books and resources. There is an excellent book called *Dyslexia at College* (see the booklist in Appendix B).

Many students with dyslexia study successfully in further and higher education – you can too. Adults can also study part time at many institutions and through the Open University. If you run into any difficulties, don't necessarily put them down to dyslexia. Talk to the tutor and the other students – it may be that everyone is finding it difficult!

Administrative issues

Signing up for courses, exams, field trips.
Knowing who to go to for what.

Possible solutions

- Lists and flowcharts
- Card index
- Personal mentor

Organizing studies

Planning; knowing when and where something
happens; knowing where rooms are; meeting
deadlines.

Possible solutions

- Wall charts and timetables
- Coloured labels and files
- Diaries
- Electronic organizer
- Negotiate for quiet workspace
- Ask for more time

Volume and pressure of work

Prioritizing. Getting help.

Possible solutions

- New list at the start of each day
- Card index of places to go for help
- Eating properly and getting exercise
- Chunking
- Taking breaks

Figure 12.2 Some ideas for coping at college

Study skills and concentration

Coping with reading; experiments and surveys; field or lab work; reading instructions; writing reports; coping with background noise and interruptions; working online.

Possible solutions

- Colour coding
- Filing trays and boxes
- Highlighting
- Using mind maps and spider diagrams
- Using templates, using the Student Support Service
- Referring to the book *Dyslexia at College*

Time

Knowing how long it takes to do something; getting to the right place at the right time; getting the right book at the right time.

Possible solutions

- Digital watch
- Mobile phone facilities
- Electronic reminders on computer
- Tell someone exactly how long it took you

Independent living

Organizing your food, your money, your washing.

Possible solutions

- Many ideas in Chapter 7

Attitudes

Coping with lecturers and tutors who are not meeting your needs.

Possible solutions

- Useful phrases to engage their understanding.

Workplace issues for employees and employers

Don't skip this section if you are not 'employed'. Working at home, looking after children or parents, doing voluntary work or working in retirement – all involve responsibilities, planning, organization and so on. There's something here for you.

About *Access to Work*

Dyslexic people can take advantage of *Access to Work* (or A2W), a government scheme to meet some costs of support at work. You may be able to get *Access to Work* if you are in a paid job, unemployed and about to start a job or self-employed. The scheme details may change from time to time but you can get the up-to-date information from your local Job Centre or from a government website such as: www.direct.gov.uk.

 ACTIVITY **25**
Thinking about issues at work

Think about the things that concern you at work. You may:
- choose work that doesn't involve too much writing;
- get more easily stressed by deadlines for reports;
- worry about writing and spelling;
- be easily distracted by noise and activity;
- feel concerned that someone who doesn't understand dyslexia may find out about yours.

Which of these are you concerned about?
What don't you like doing and what do you try to avoid?

Activity 25—*continued*

Now think about a few things that you are good at in your job, that you enjoy doing and that you feel confident to do. Your list might include:
- meeting and talking to other people;
- solving problems;
- finding new and better ways of doing things;
- giving informal presentations;
- being good with computer software;
- helping others.

The trick in work (and life) is to *emphasize* the things you are good at and use these strengths to help you with the things that give you problems. So use this book and the people close to you to help you identify your strengths.

In Chapters 5 to 10 we've introduced lots of ideas and strategies that we know work for dyslexic adults. You can adapt these for use in your work depending on your tasks and responsibilities. We hope you'll try them . . . if you haven't already. In Chapter 11 we've covered some useful technology. We hope you'll consider some of this too.

Dyslexia can give rise to problems at work in seven broad areas:
- Procedures – the order in which things should be done.
- Organization – planning.
- Workload – coping with the amount of work.
- Literacy – filing, reading, writing, spelling.
- Time – how long things take and coping with deadlines.
- Concentration – coping with noise and interruptions.
- Attitudes of others – not recognizing your ability.

ACTIVITY 26
Strategies and ideas for the workplace

Look at each of the seven headings in Figure 12.3. Highlight any tasks that you have to do in your work. Add any that are specific to your particular work that are not on the list. Think about some strategies you could use. Put a circle round those you'd like to try . . . and try them.

In Figure 12.3 we have listed some common tasks under each of these headings and suggested some strategies you can use.

On training courses
What are the possible issues?
- having to present something in a group;
- having to read something quickly;
- having to write something.

You can:
- ask for reading material in advance;
- volunteer to lead a discussion and then ask someone else to act as note-taker;
- in discussions or lectures you could explain that you work better if you don't have to take notes, so you would like agreement to make recordings;
- ask others to summarize briefly what they are going to do, e.g. 'could you please take us through the programme first?'. This avoids the surprise of a new topic and associated jargon;
- ask the trainer to sum up if necessary.

After the course, consider offering to give your colleagues a summary. You can ask for a copy of any PowerPoint presentation or relevant notes to help you.

Tasks and issues at work	Strategies (for more details refer back to Chapters 5–7)
Procedures Remembering the order you have to do things in; remembering who has responsibility for what	• Lists and flow charts
Organization Planning; knowing when and where something happens; knowing where things are	• Wall charts and timetables • Coloured labels and files • Mind maps • Trade or swap tasks with others
Workload Prioritizing; delegating	• New lists at the start of each day
Literacy issues Filing; reading instructions; writing and reading reports	• Colour coding filing trays and boxes. • Highlighting • Using mind maps • Using templates and models • Using a secretary or PA
Time Knowing how long it takes to do something; getting to the right place at the right time	• Digital watch • Mobile phone or computer facilities
Concentration Coping with background noise and interruptions	• Negotiate for a quiet work area. • Move to unoccupied rooms occasionally.
Attitudes Coping with colleagues who do not understand dyslexia; being called untidy, careless or disorganized	• Useful phrases to help others understand • Seeking help from an appropriate colleague if attitudes become unhelpful

Figure 12.3 Some ideas for coping in the workplace

Should you tell work colleagues about your dyslexia?

Dyslexia is becoming better understood but there are still misconceptions about the subject, so you need to make a judgement about who you tell. Discuss it with someone whose opinion you trust first.

You can just make your *needs* known. Dyslexia is a label and labels can be misleading. Dyslexia is idiosyncratic – each person has a different set of strengths and difficulties just like everyone does. No two people experience dyslexia in the same way.

Words and phrases to help you

Most of us find it hard to say how we would like to be treated. We may not be able to find the right words in a given situation. It helps to have some phrases ready. You could keep them handy in a notebook. Practise saying them until you feel comfortable with them and can summon them up easily. Try using or adapting the suggestions in Figure 12.4. Add any others you find useful.

Supporting others

You're unlikely to be the only dyslexic person you know. One in 10 people have some dyslexic difficulties – for one in 20, the difficulties can be quite problematic. In a large family there may be several affected in some way because dyslexia has a genetic basis. If you work with 50 people, you can expect to find about five with similar difficulties. *You* can help them because you have some understanding of their feelings and frustrations.

If you have a dyslexic employee, then you can use all the ideas suggested in this chapter and Chapter 4. Talk their tasks through with them so that, together, you can identify the appropriate support and strategies.

Look out for local support groups – these will include parents, dyslexic young people and adults. The British Dyslexia Association keeps a list and your local library may have details. You can also try the internet. Often there are regular meetings with speakers on a range of subjects. We strongly encourage you to seek out your local group. You will find people who understand, who are non-judgemental – a safe environment to share your problems and try things out. Groups often have an advice line run by volunteers. Your own expertise will be invaluable to them too.

Epilogue: Where do you go from here?

Wherever you want to go!! There is such a lot that you can do to achieve your aims. We hope you have already discovered some new ideas in this book. If you don't feel confident about something, you should now realize that there are many ways you can maximize your potential:

- Decide what it is you want to do.
- Then identify the strategies that are going to get you there.

Over the years you may have been given inappropriate or very little help to overcome your difficulties. Don't give yourself a hard time because you may have been given the wrong tools – the wrong approach for *you*.

The very fact that you are reading this book is testimony to your persistence and determination, which are two of the most important characteristics of success.

Moreover, the way you think as a dyslexic adult can be a bonus because it is often creative and holistic. These are talents that can give you a head start in new ways of looking at yourself and the world.

☺ It may not look like it but my workspace is organized the way I work best.

☺ I am more effective when I talk it through and someone else makes notes.

☺ My spelling is unreliable – is correct spelling important for this?

☺ My spelling is creative – it would be useful if you could check it.

☺ I need some extra time to get my head around this.

☺ It really helps when you give an outline of what you are going to do first.

☺ Please can you send me everything electronically so I can reformat if I need to?

☺ Can you write that down for me?

☺ Just a moment while I write that down.

☺ Can I double check that with you?

☺ Are those instructions written down anywhere? I would find that really useful.

☺ A short 1–1 session on that would be really useful.

☺ Can I have a photocopy of that?

☺ That's useful – please will you send that to me in an email?

☺ Your encouragement makes a lot of difference. I really value your feedback.

Now some of your own:

☺ _____

☺ _____

Figure 12.4 Some useful phrases

We weren't expecting you to read this book from cover to cover. You may have dipped into it over a period of days, months, even years. You may have come straight to this page to see how it all ends! Now you are here . . .

Pause for a moment

Since starting to read this book:
- What have you tried? What do you want to try?
- What has been a useful learning experience?
- What might you do next?

When we finished writing this book we reflected on all the people with dyslexia we have met over the years. We thought about some of their qualities that seemed to stand out, the positive aspects of dyslexia that we have mentioned throughout this book. Figure 12.5 is a collection of the adjectives that come to mind.

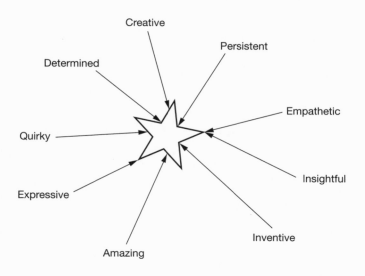

... and having a sense of humour and strong sense of achievement

Figure 12.5 Words that describe you

So we dedicate this book to all those we've known
who have inspired us to write it.

Appendix A

Checklist for dyslexia

If you think you might be dyslexic, this checklist is for you to work through. You will find others on a number of websites but this one is a good start. It includes a range of questions that help identify dyslexia-type difficulties. Think carefully, but not for too long, about your answers. You might find it useful to ask other people who know you well to comment or help you complete the form.

Please tick the appropriate boxes and add any comments that come to mind as you reflect on each section. There is a printable version on the website.

Thinking back over your early years, do you remember . . .	Yes	No	Some-times
Being later in learning to read or write than others?			
Not wanting to read aloud in class?			
Finding it hard to memorize spellings?			
Misreading numbers or writing them incorrectly?			
Having difficulty learning multiplication tables?			
Anything else you remember: e.g. clumsiness, lack of coordination in ball games, difficulty with organization?			

When you are reading, do you often . . .	Yes	No	Some-times
Misread or misinterpret a passage?			
Find reading a difficult and slow process?			
Only make sense of a passage by rereading it several times?			
Take a long time to scan a passage for the main point?			
Anything else about your reading such as coping with reading new and unfamiliar words?			

When you are writing, do you . . .	Yes	No	Some-times
Find organizing ideas on paper more difficult than explaining them verbally?			
Find it hard to listen and take notes at the same time?			
Find it hard to copy things accurately?			
Struggle to remember the word you want to describe or name something?			
Miss out letters or parts (syllables) of words?			
Confuse or reverse letters in a word (e.g. b/d, f/t, n/v)?			
Anything else about your writing such as being uneven or untidy?			

In your everyday life now, do you find yourself generally . . .	Yes	No	Some-times
Avoiding reading?			
Avoiding writing?			
Having difficulty when filling in forms?			
Mispronouncing common words?			
Tending to get telephone numbers mixed up?			
Confusing dates and missing appointments?			
Not being able to find the right word for something?			
Needing written reminders for everything and still forgetting?			
Having difficulty organizing your paperwork?			
Confusing left and right?			
Dreading being given verbal instructions?			
Are your difficulties shared by other family members?			

Interpreting your answers

If you ticked 'Yes' or 'Sometimes' to most of the questions in one or more of the sections, you may be dyslexic.

You are likely to find many of the ideas and strategies in this book useful.

There are a number of helplines, both local and national, available for you to discuss dyslexia with someone. You can start by contacting the organizations listed in Appendix C.

If you have ticked 'No' more often than 'Yes'.

Many people experience some of these difficulties, especially when they are under pressure. They may arise from many different sources such as previous school experiences, hearing problems or a change in language. You may not be dyslexic or you may be mildly dyslexic. But you will still find some ideas in this book useful.

Appendix B

Useful and interesting books

General interest for dyslexic adults

That's the Way I Think: Dyslexia, dyspraxia and ADHD explained. David Grant (Routledge, 2nd edn, 2010).
   This edition has been revised and enlarged. Dr Grant deals with the problems of dyslexia, dyspraxia and ADHD in an informal way making it eminently readable.

Dyslexia: How to Detect and Manage Dyslexia: A reference and resource manual. Philomena Ott (Heinemann, 1997).
   A good overall reference and resource.

Dyslexia: A hundred years on. T.R. Miles and Elaine Miles (Open University Press, 2nd edn, 1999).
   A good general overview of the field, especially interesting to teachers.

In the Mind's Eye. Thomas G. West (Prometheus, 2nd edn, 2009).
   An exploration of the creative side of dyslexia.

Dyslexia, How Would I cope? Michael Ryden (Jessica Kingsley, 1997).
   Written from personal experience, this book clearly describes and illustrates how written communication can appear to a dyslexic person.

Specific areas of interest

Planning and organization

The Mind Map Book: Unlock your creativity, boost your memory, change your life. Tony Buzan (BBC Active, 2009).

Tony Buzan is the inventor of Mind Maps and *The Mind Map Book* is the original and best book on how to use them effectively in your own life. There are also several downloadable videos on how to mind map to be found on the internet.

Handwriting

Improve Your Handwriting. Rosemary Sassoon (Teach Yourself Books, 2010).
A practical guide to handwriting problems and strategies.

Spelling dictionary

The Ace Spelling Dictionary. David Moseley (LDA, 2009).
This dictionary is arranged on sounds rather than actual spellings. You identify the first sound of the word and follow the clear instructions.

Spelling

How to Manage Spelling Successfully. Philomena Ott (Routledge, 2007).
Readers will find this practical and comprehensive guide to spelling invaluable.

Grammar

Rediscover Grammar. David Crystal (Longman, 3rd edn, 2004).
A really entertaining book that starts from scratch.

Numbers and maths

Dealing with Dyscalculia: Sum hope. Steve Chinn (Souvenir Press Ltd, revised and enlarged edition, 2007).
Steve Chinn clearly explains the basic principles of mathematics, how they can be used in various situations, and how numbers are not threatening and so begin to make sense.

Punctuation

Penguin English Guide to Punctuation. R.L. Trask (Penguin Books, 1997).
A short helpful guide.

The internet

Rough Guide to the Internet. Peter Buckley and Duncan Clark (Rough Guides, 14th edn, 2009).
Regularly updated. Good, basic guide written in plain English.

Books for students

Dyslexia at College. Liz du Pre, T.R. Miles and D.E. Gilroy (Routledge, 3rd edn, 2007).
Really sound advice for anyone thinking of going to college. Don't try to read it all in one go.

Study skills

The Study Skills Handbook. Stella Cottrell (Palgrave, 3rd edn, 2008).
An excellent book for all students. Well presented and includes lots of ideas for tackling a range of difficulties and improving study skills.

In the workplace

Dyslexia in the Workplace: An introductory guide. Diane Bartlett, Sylvia Moody and Katherine Kindersley (Wiley-Blackwell, 2nd edn, 2010).
A comprehensive guide to how dyslexic adults in employment can improve their skills, and how their employers and other professionals can help.

Footnote

A particularly helpful documentary was made by BBC3 in November 2010 about Kara Tointon and her experiences of dyslexia: *Don't Call Me Stupid.* The programme is available to view here: www.workingwithdyslexia.com/news/.

Appendix C

Useful addresses

Always check the organization's website for up-to-date information.

British Dyslexia Association

Unit 8 Bracknell Beeches
Old Bracknell Lane
Bracknell RG12 7BW
 Tel: 0845 251 9003
 Fax: 0845 251 9005
 Helpline: 0845 251 9002
 Website: www.bdadyslexia.org.uk
Has some useful fact sheets for adults. Many local branches, some of which have adult groups. Useful for assessments and learning skills support. A lot of information is available from the website.

Dyslexia Action

Egham Centre
Park House
Wick Road
Egham
Surrey TW20 0HH
 Tel: 01784 222 300
 Fax: 01784 222 333
 Email: info@dyslexiaaction.org.uk
 Website: www.dyslexiaaction.org.uk/
Offers tuition and assessments for all ages throughout the UK. There are many local organizations also offering tuition and assessment. Look in your local library or phone book for details.

Adult Dyslexia Organization
Ground Floor
Secker House
Minet Road
Loughborough Estate
London SW9 7TP
    Helpline: 020 7924 9559
    Email: dyslexiahq@dial.pipex.com
    Admin: 020 7207 3911
    Admin email: ado.dns@dial.pipex.com
    Website: www.adult-dyslexia.org/
A helpful, professional and friendly organization for adults who
have dyslexia, used for professionals and others with an
interest in adults. Publishes newsletters, fact sheets, guidance
notes and so on, and runs meetings and conferences.
Quickest route to their website is probably through the BDA
website.

iansyst
Fen House
Fen Road
Cambridge CB4 1UN
    Tel: 01223 42 01 01
    Email: customer.services@iansyst.co.uk
    Website: http://iansyst.com
National and international experts in assistive technology
solutions, particularly for dyslexics. Very helpful organization
that can help you to decide on the best computer packages
for you.

The Dyslexia Association of Ireland
Suffolk Chambers
1 Suffolk Street
Dublin 2
    Tel: 01 6790276
    Fax: 01 6790273
    Email: info@dyslexia.ie

International Dyslexia Association (USA and affiliated countries)

40 York Rd, 4th Floor
Baltimore
MD 21204
USA
    Tel: (410) 296–0232
    Fax: (410) 321–5069
    Website: www.interdys.org
A non-profit, scientific, and educational organization dedicated to the study and treatment of the learning disability, dyslexia.

Australia and New Zealand

Specific Learning Disabilities Federation (SPELD) is a non-profit organization that provides advice and services to children and adults with specific learning difficulties, such as dyslexia. It has member associations throughout Australia and New Zealand:

SPELD in Australia

Dyslexia-SPELD Foundation WA Inc.
Postal Address:
PO Box 409
South Perth WA 6951
    Tel: (08) 9217 2500
    Fax: (08) 9217 2599
    Email: support@dsf.net.au
    Website: www.auspeld.org.au
Each state has its own SPELD organization.

SPELD NZ

The Langham
83 Symonds Street
Auckland 1010
    Tel in NZ: 0800 773 536

 See our website for links to these organizations.

Appendix D

Glossary

An explanation of words in this book that you may not have come across before. Most of these words are explained where they occur in the main text.

Accommodations Allowances made in examinations such as extra time. Sometimes called 'concessions'.

Alphabetic strategy According to Frith, the second stage of learning to read – by sounding out the letters.

Assessment An interview and a series of tests designed to identify dyslexia and your strengths.

Asymmetric Something that isn't symmetric – see 'symmetric'.

Auditory To do with hearing.

Automaticity The ability to do things automatically.

Blend Two or more consonant sounds that run together such as br, pl, rt.

Cerebellum The section at the lower back of the brain that is responsible for things we do automatically. Often referred to as the brain's 'auto-pilot'.

Chunking What smart dyslexics do – break things (tasks, words, sentences etc.) down into manageable amounts.

Coding Transferring word sounds into letters and words.

Cognitive ability A measure of learning skills such as memory, phonological awareness and fluency.

Cognitive learning style How you think and approach your learning.

Coloured overlays See Mears-Irlen overlays.

Compensated dyslexic A dyslexic person whose literacy and numeracy attainment is reasonable because of good strategies. They may still have considerable difficulties.

Comprehension What you understand about a piece of text you have read.

Concessions Allowances made in examinations such as extra time. More usually called *accommodations* these days.

Concrete example An example that you can readily identify with; explains a concept.

Consonant 21 of the 26 letters of the alphabet – those that are not vowels (a, e, i, o, u).

Cuisenaire rods Small coloured sticks that have a different colour for each length. Used for getting the feel of quantity.

Decoding Taking the letters or groups of letters and translating into sounds to make words.

Denominator In maths, the bottom number of a fraction: e.g. in 1/2 the 2 is the denominator.

Diagnosis In dyslexia a diagnosis is made on the basis of cognitive skills being less well developed. This is an identification of dyslexia.

Dyscalculia A difficulty with maths that is unexpected, usually around concepts of numbers and quantity. Some people with dyslexia are affected.

Dyslexia A specific learning difficulty.

Dyslexia learning style Dyslexics tend to think holistically, intuitively and are creative.

Dyspraxia Difficulties with planning, organization and movement.

Electronic dictionary Available as pocket-sized objects – you can look up the meaning or spelling of a word without using a book.

Fluency The ability of the brain to do or think something over and over and more and more quickly without being conscious of it.

Font The style of letters used in print.

Frontal lobe The front part of the brain that deals with thinking, planning and conceptualization.

General intellectual ability A measure of ability made by combining the results of verbal and non-verbal reasoning tests.

Genes (genetics) Parts of a chromosome that carry the code for development of living things (the study of genes).

Gypsy method A method of multiplying using the fingers of both hands explained on the website. It is particularly useful for 6–10 times tables.

Hemisphere One half of a sphere. One half of the brain.

Holistic, holistically Taking an overall approach. Seeing things as a whole.

Intuitive colorimeter An instrument used by an optometrist to find the best colour light to help prevent print blurring or distorting.

Kinaesthetic learning Learning by doing.

Literacy Ability to read and write.

Logographic strategy According to Frith, the first stage of learning to read – by recognizing the look of a word.

Mears-Irlen overlays Coloured sheets of plastic that can help to stabilize print and make it more comfortable to read.

Metacognition Understanding the way you learn.

Mind map A diagram used to represent words, ideas, or tasks.

Mnemonic A trick for remembering things. Pronounced 'nemonic', the m is silent.

Motor skills Skills that involve movement such as catching a ball.

Multi-sensory learning Employing more than one sense when you learn – it helps to learn things using many senses.

Needs assessment An opportunity to be tested by an expert to see what your needs are and what solutions might be useful.

Neurological To do with the body's nervous system, especially the brain.

Neuroscience The study of how the brain functions.

Non-transparent language A language like English where there is little correspondence between speech sounds and letters do not correspond regularly.

Onset and rime The onset is the first sound of a word or syllable. The rime is the second sound.

Optometrist A professional practitioner qualified to examine eyes and prescribe treatment such as spectacles, contact lenses etc. Often referred to as opticians.

Orthographic strategy According to Frith, the third stage of learning to read – recognizing chunks of words and relating them to sounds.

Paired reading A strategy of reading alternately with a good reader helps to improve fluency and confidence.

Percentile The result of a test or tests quoted as the level you have reached being higher than that percentage of people.

Phoneme A single speech unit: sh-ee-p has three phonemes.

Phonological Relating to language sounds.

Phonology The study of sounds that are found in language. This means the sounds used when you speak rather than sounds made when you scream, laugh or cough.

Psychometric tests Tests that measure all aspects of mental ability: personality, intelligence, aptitude etc.

Readability level An easily calculated measure of the degree of difficulty of a passage of text.

Reading age An indication of a child's reading skills. It can be above, the same as or below their actual age.

Read-out facility Text to speech packages for the computer – see Chapter 9.

Right brained Over-generalized description for the creative skills.

Scanning, scanners A non-invasive method of observing what is happening in internal organs such as the brain. Also, equipment that reads text into a computer.

Scotopic A misnomer for visual discomfort not caused by sensitivity or an eye defect.

Screening Short tests and/or an interview with a specialist to see if you have dyslexic traits, before going for a full assessment.

Self-esteem Overall evaluation of your worth.

Sensory learning style The sense(s) you use most when you learn.

Sequencing Putting things in a specific order, e.g. alphabetical order.

Software Computer programs that do real work for you, for example: word processors such as *Word*, spreadsheets such as *Excel*, planning tools such as *Inspiration*.

Standard score Test results that have been recalculated so that they can be compared to the performance of a particular group and also across a range of different tests.

Syllable Part of a word said with one single effort of the voice. So 'sheep' has only one syllable (compare this with a 'phoneme' as described above).

Symmetric An object where each side of the middle line is a mirror image.

Thesaurus A kind of dictionary where words are grouped together according to similar meanings.

Tracking How the eye follows a line of print across a page.

Transparent language A language where the letters or groups of letters always represent the same sound, e.g. Italian.

Visual To do with seeing.

Visual loop A model for the brain processing visual information.

Vowel The letters of the alphabet that are not consonants: a, e, i, o, u – sometimes y.

Index